8.03 17 1/53

TRANSFERED TO MAIN 6/99

✓ FD 12|87 ⑥

✓ FD 6/28 ①

Exorcism

Exorcism

Possession or Obsession?

Richard Deutch

Foreword by the
Reverend Christopher Neil-Smith

Bachman & Turner: London

Bachman & Turner
45 Calthorpe Street
London WC1 0HH

© Richard Deutch 1975

First published 1975

ISBN 0 85974 042 0

Computer typeset by Input Typesetting Ltd,
4 Valentine Place, London S.E.1.
Printed in Great Britain by
Lowe & Brydone (Printers) Ltd, Thetford, Norfolk

This book is

for Helene Hodge, adept, teacher, and one whom I presume to call friend;

for Jacque Rhode, whose criticisms were sometimes maddening but always accurate, which made them sometimes all the more maddening, and without whose love and concern I would not have lived to write it;

and for anyone who has ever suffered psychic attack.

Contents

Foreword by the
Reverend Christopher Neil-Smith

Richard Deutch when he was writing this book was a resident parishioner of mine – a self styled materialistic agnostic and lapsed Catholic – so similar to another author parishioner who calls himself an Anglo agnostic.

No doubt you might expect a Theologian to write on a subject like 'exorcism' but strange though it may seem it is only recently that 65 academic Theologians* (bishops and priests) have written an Open Letter decrying or denying the practice of exorcism. It is therefore all the more surprising that a book on 'exorcism' should come from the pen of a materialistic agnostic – a quite startling reversal of his and their expected roles. That is what makes this book so arresting and stimulating – it relates to the unexpected!

Academics often claim that they are open-minded and open-ended but these Theologians appear to have closed their minds to the possibility of exorcism by preconceived and abstract ideas quite unrelated to experience. In contrast, we have here an author from a totally different standpoint and with a scant regard for Church formularies who has come to recognise the significance of exorcism for himself as a fact of human experience.

Richard is also an academic steeped in Rationalist philosophy – once a university lecturer in the USA yet strangely convinced by his own experience of the reality of witchcraft and evil forces. He talks of 'sane' exorcism and expresses a well balanced attitude to what is sometimes thought to be hysterical. He speaks from a versatile experience – actor, author and poet – a man with deep sensitivity and perceptive awareness who traverses the realms of the spiritual

* *The Times*, 15 May 1975.

9

world with a natural propensity so singularly lacking in some religious people. Some people assert that the age of reason in the past decade has changed into an age of superstition. Is it purely superstition or is it not a revival of the supernatural? Not long ago, I was asked to open a Debate at a University on the motion 'This house believes in supernatural forces' and the seconder to the motion was the High Priest of a witch coven. In spite of the fact that students are often considered atheistic and rational, this motion was passed with a substantial majority. This clearly reflects the fact that there has been a 'wind of change' towards the supernatural in the past decade but not necessarily in its traditional form. For instance, it is held that there are over four hundred Black Magic groups in this country and at least one in every university. According to a *Daily Mirror* survey* there are 40,000 witches in this country – a fact which cannot be lightly or jokingly disregarded.

In this book, Richard makes a direct challenge to the Church to undertake exorcism and not to disregard it or decry it. I have had several confrontations with him over witchcraft and exorcism and he has left me with *no* illusion about the 'powers' and forces involved. This book speaks to witches black and white with whom Richard is familiar through his own initiation; it speaks to lapsed Catholics who will recognise familiar rituals; it speaks to those who feel their need for exorcism and like Richard seek for an exorcist. It may well speak to you.

Christopher Neil-Smith
Author of *The Exorcist and the Possessed*

---

* *Daily Mirror*, 28 February 1972.

PART I
Did you say exorcise or exercise?

An Anglican minister remarked to me recently that whereas in the Freud-ridden twenties the in-thing to say was 'As I was telling my analyst the other day . . .' the new cocktail party *bon mot* is likely to be prefaced by 'As I was saying to my exorcist . . .' The novel and film *The Exorcist,* which came very close to being a documentary of an actual case of possession, made, to paraphrase a paraphrase, a new cult of the occult, and a plethora of books and movies and television interviews followed. The subject became hot as hell, so to speak, and it has not cooled down. Headlines such as 'SHE WAS A SLAVE TO PRIESTS OF SATAN' continue to appear in the more slavering banner headlines of the more libidinous newspapers, and on at least one occassion an attempted exorcism resulted in a man murdering his wife.

The church has responded by seriously considering the banishment of exorcism from the liturgy. As Christ was himself a powerful exorcist and passed this power on to his disciples, who practised exorcism frequently (see Part II), one wonders what is to be left of so-called Christianity if this line of reasoning is followed to its logical conclusion. If one of the

11

faithful chokes on a piece of bread, will bishops then decide that Jesus was acting dangerously when he handed out loaves and fishes? Will they consider eliminating the Eucharist? The fact is that exorcism is a reality which will not be dismissed, and the church is shirking its responsibility in failing to provide trained exorcists and spiritual guides in an extremely dangerous field.

Is exorcism therapeutic or is it simply a vestigial form of superstitious hysteria? The question is certainly valid and has been discussed recently by psychologists, theologians and even those who have practised exorcism. This book argues that exorcism is indeed a potent form of therapy, but only justifiable when every other possible treatment has been tried and proved ineffectual. A behavioural therapist, who is also interested and knowledgeable in the occult, remarked to me recently, 'No one is an expert in this field'. This is true partly because no two cases involving exorcism are exactly alike. Certain patterns are traceable; certain dogmatized rituals are known to have worked (and to have failed). But the personal make-up of the patient is always different, making the problem of obsession or possession a little bit intricate, to say the least.

The cases against exorcism come from a remarkable spectrum of people: Baroness Summerskill, a Labour peer, proposed to the House of Lords that exorcists be legally obliged to justify their practice; the psychology correspondent Robert Shields has presented an excellently balanced protest against exorcism; Maxine Sanders, a Witch Queen, says that the practice is far too widespread and used indiscriminately; and the Reverend Brian Hebblethwaite, Fellow of Queens' College, Cambridge, accuses even Jesus of superstition, of having been a phoney exorcist who 'shared that ancient world-view' * that exorcism was a valid form of curing spiritual disease. The last source of protest is, to me, shocking.

Sir Martin Roth, president of the Royal College of Psychiatrics, has spoken of an incipient 'spirit possession spreading by contagion' due to the renewed interest in exorcism and added, 'One person screaming hysterically can

* *News of the World*, 27 April 1975.

set off another'.* Dr William Sargent, author of the very eloquent argument against the occult in general, *The Mind Possessed,* remarked,

> There could be an epidemic of religious fervour as there was in Wesley's time, with clergymen preaching hellfire and damnation or some modern equivalent. But the danger is that, once people lose faith, they are open to influence by other gods not quite so benevolent.

Dr Sargeant is referring to the failure of the orthodox churches to provide a means to 'relieve emotion'; he is commenting on the resultant reborn interest in the occult and revivalism as practised in the United States. This latter Elmer Gantry 'religion' was regarded by no less controversial a figure than Aleister Crowley as the most debased form of Black Magic. The prospect of widespread cultist hysteria is not so remote as one would like to think: the brutal murder of Christine Taylor by her husband, described by his friends as 'a stable, intelligent, hard-working young man with no signs of mental illness', brought to public attention the dangers of both revivalism and incompetent, premature and ill-advised exorcism. The fact that Taylor's temporary insanity had been brought about by his participation in fundamentalist prayer meetings some time before he was exorcised seemed to escape the attention of the press, whose reporters were still mesmerized by the selling power of anything connectable with *The Exorcist.*

But the Taylor case is a most dramatic illustration of two of the dangers common to the practice of exorcism. The rite of exorcism should never be performed until the patient has seen a GP, or specialist, and a psychiatrist; an encephalograph should be insisted upon. There are times when a truly disturbed person needs immediate spiritual attention, and methods for giving it appear in Part IV of this book; but in general the no doubt well-meaning 'exorcists' who worked on Michael Taylor were ill-advised in not taking him first to a doctor. Secondly, an exorcism, once it is undertaken, *must never*

* The dangerous art of exorcism,' *Sunday Times,* 27 April 1975.

13

be abandoned until it is concluded. Nor should the patient be left alone to get into mischief – or murder – until the ritual has been deemed complete by a trained exorcist. Several examples of the necessity for this will be given in some case histories later on.

But what is exorcism, precisely? And should it ever be performed at all?

Any sane approach to the subject should first of all recognize that exorcism is not an alternative to medicine or psychiatry. It is a method of treatment to be undertaken when both these have failed.

In a pamphlet which is quoted extensively throughout this book,* a commission of Roman Catholic and Anglican priests defined exorcism as 'the binding of evil powers by the triumph of Christ Jesus, through the application of the power demonstrated by that triumph, in and by his Church'. Obviously, this is intended to apply exclusively to Christian exorcism. But 'the binding of evil powers' seems a good starting point for a definition of exorcism as practised by other religions and lay exorcists. Another phrase from the same pamphlet is apposite: for the purposes of this book I shall define exorcism as an attempt to correct, by ritualistic means, 'a distortion of right orderliness'. This may involve people, places or things.

As Dion Fortune pointed out, any action is ritualistic where the agent is conscious of his own will and intent; so dissolving an aspirin in water to 'exorcise' a headache may be considered a form of ritual and rightly. The sensationalist depiction in *The Exorcist* of Max Von Sydow slobbering holy water all over a little girl possessed by a demon entity is relatively rare but by no means entirely fictional, as documented evidence has all too often shown. Joan Grant, author of *Winged Pharaoh* and various other books, said,

> People came to me expecting me to tell them that in a previous incarnation they were Cleopatra, or something, and their problems date from some mistake they made

* *Exorcism. The Findings of A Commission by the Bishop of Exeter*, SPCK, 1975 edn.

14

when they were alive in ancient Egypt. Actually, their problem is usually much more simple and up-to-date. 'My mother didn't love me,' they say. 'No, she didn't,' I say. 'Why should she have? Now why don't you just get on with it?'

This, too, is a form of exorcism. In *Winged Pharaoh* we are presented with a 'fictional' society in which spiritual leaders and medicinal healers work together. Anaesthetics are unnecessary, because priests trained in astral travel draw the spirit out of the patient's body before the operation. This practice, an ancient one, has just recently resurfaced as hypnotism, once a scientific bugaboo but now widely respected. If the question of exorcism is to be put into any rational perspective at all, it must be recognized that man has certain spiritual needs, certain fears, which cannot be dealt with by ordinary practices of medicine or psychiatry. Until this is appreciated, we shall always be in danger of exorcisms being performed exclusively by a lunatic fringe. The aim of this book is to open minds closed to the subject and to foster responsible attitudes towards a practice which pre-dates Christianity by thousands of years, suddenly re-appearing not with a whimper but a bang. It will not go away simply because we shut our eyes to it.

The cynics – I am thinking now of those psychoanalysts who, professing to care about the human condition, deny it its spirituality – must be made to understand that whether or not they feel exorcism *ought* to be practised, it *will* be. Neil-Smith* quotes a United States congressional report which states that in cases concerning 'the needs and resources of the mentally ill' 42 per cent of the disturbed people went to their clergymen, but only 18 per cent consulted psychiatrists. If Lady Summerskill should ever succeed in passing through a Bill to outlaw exorcism, she would only be instigating a repeat performance of the Medieval Witch hunts I describe in Part II. Exorcism would not cease to be performed. It would merely go underground and probably suffer corruption in the process. Exorcism, as I have defined it, does work; not always,

* *The Exorcist and the Possessed*, New York: Pinnacle Books, 1974, p. 3.

but then neither do the more orthodox and licensed means of dealing with distressed persons. The fact that it does work, sometimes with dramatic success, is reason enough to take it seriously.

This leads us to a fascinating but ultimately unanswerable – and, in the long run, irrelevant – question: is a person who feels he is possessed in fact suffering disturbance from an 'exterior' invading entity existing outside himself, or is he the victim of his own 'interior' problems, environmental, chemical, genetic, circumstantial or whatever? The latter possibility should be explored first unless in an obvious emergency. If the person is levitating dangerously or speaking a language he has never studied, reciting a few prayers while someone else telephones for assistance may not help but 'it couldn't hurt'. My own thesis is that either situation – mental or physical imbalance or genuine psychic disturbance coming from another source – can exist independently but the former can seriously increase the chances of the latter. A spirit entity, be it a discarnate human soul, a true spirit, or an externalized demon of the patient's own creation, will find a mentally or physically weakened subject easier prey for possession than one who is happy and sound. And demons, like anybody else, tend to do things the easy way if they can.

Your own beliefs about spirits and demonology, your experience of psychic phenomena, will determine how much you will accept this attitude. But no psychoanalyst with a dossier on the subject can deny that exorcism has been helpful in clearing up 'psychic bugs' on some occasions, wherever they come from. He would certainly have Jung to contend with if he managed to achieve this degree of narrow-mindedness, which is known in American academics as Hardening of the Categories.

Like it or not, scientifically documented phenomena such as ghosts, ESP, haunted houses, psychokinesis or poltergeists, do indicate indisputably that the mind has certain powers which we have yet to explain or define and may even suggest to the more open-minded that discarnate or spirit entities do exist independently of what we call 'ourselves'. They may even exist independently of what we have the impudence to call 'the

16

physical world', we who haven't the slightest notion of what sort of creatures may exist on the ocean floor. Medical science – as well as psychiatry, philosophy and theology – has too often been guilty of assuming that by merely naming a syndrome one has somehow got control over it. 'Cancer' is a perfect example. 'Phobia' is another. Watching *The Exorcist* with Neil-Smith we came to a particularly chilling scene in which the possessed girl is hypnotized by a psychiatrist, whose initial attitude towards the whole problem is that he is slightly less omniscient than Yehovah Adonai. The language he and the medical doctor also present were using in attempting to describe the symptoms was absolute double-talk, and Neil-Smith suddenly burst into laughter. I had seen the movie before, but the humour of the scene hadn't struck me. 'And the more they talk like that,' I said, 'the worse it gets.'

When we enter the realm of the psyche we are facing the Unknown: sometimes, but not always, a pretty sight. We must be prepared for phenomena we do not at present and may never understand completely. To quote Dion Fortune again, what we want is results, not explanations.

The question persists, however, and like a possessing entity will not be driven away. What is it precisely that one exorcises? What *is* evil? Neil-Smith, a practical man, describes evil as 'bad vibrations'. The *Oxford English Dictionary* gives us as good a definition as any when it describes evil first as bad in a positive sense, then as bad in a privative sense. Hemingway once defined 'bad' as that which makes you feel bad, and 'good' as what makes you feel good – and this is nowhere near as simplistic as it sounds. The occultist believes in the law of karma, or universal justice-as-an-inevitability. Evil may for present purposes be defined as a 'distortion of right orderliness'. Thus defined, illness is an evil; any action which does positive or privative harm to another is an evil; any action which does harm to oneself is evil. When Aleister Crowley said 'Do What Thou Wilt shall be the whole of the Law,' he added, 'Love is the Law: Love under Will.' 'Love under Will' is an expression of that 'right orderliness' which, when disturbed, it is the duty of the exorcist to set right. Many formulae for ritual exorcism have been compiled in this book, but the essence of exorcism is contained in these words.

I have named this book *Exorcism: Obsession or Possession?* and have done so at the risk of being misunderstood by occultists, who may take 'obsession' to mean a psychic disturbance caused by an entity which has not in fact entered 'into' the patient but has besieged his spirit in some way. In fact I meant to use the word as it has come more commonly to be understood; an unhealthy preoccupation. There is no doubt that the subject of exorcism has become precisely this, for far too many persons, and I should like to say at the outset that I (and in fact, most exorcists) disapprove of the widespread use of exorcism. No true exorcist will abuse his gift by using it when it is unnecessary. Before determining that an exorcism is necessary – unless a state of emergency obviously exists – the exorcist will prescribe every other means of deciding the nature of the problem and finding a cure. However, it is also the thesis of this book that possession does occur, and it is my hope to have provided some practical advice that may be of some help. Under no circumstances should anyone who is untrained undertake an exorcism. In England, anyway, qualified help is available in the event of a psychic disturbance, and information on how to obtain it may be found in Part IV.

There are many voices in this book, because there are many approaches to the subject. Rather than try to impose my own brand of orthodoxy (after two years as a Witch, I have decided that Witch orthodoxy is, happily, a contradiction in fact) I have allowed all manner of controversy to appear as it does actually exist. I have done this at the risk of being accused of inconsistency; exorcism is a wide-open subject, and in order to mirror it accurately one must, occasionally, be apparently inconsistent in order to fit the reportage to the subject.

In this work I have not attempted to end the controversy on the subject of exorcism, but on the contrary to stir it up so that certain questions may be, if not answered, at least illuminated. That is one reason why I asked my friend, the Reverend Neil-Smith, to write a Foreword to the book. I have not yet seen his Foreword, but am sure that as we disagree on certain points over the occasional brandy he will not miss a

18

chance to take me to task over any mistakes I have made: that is all to the good. My thanks are extended as well to the various experts in the field of exorcism and behavioural therapy who gave me their time and looked at the manuscript, correcting obvious blunders and suggesting improvements.

Exorcism is not a subject or practice that is likely to disappear in the near or even distant future; it must be met rationally and open-mindedly. Any attempt to dismiss it lightly or legislate it out of existence can be likened to the American attempt to outlaw alcohol during Prohibition: the saloons may close, but the speakeasies will open and the situation will be worse than ever.

PART II

Approaches to exorcism

1   Christian exorcism

'Now to come to speak of the driving away of evil Spirits;
it is to be known, that very few since the time of Christ
and his Apostles have rightly been driven away.'
— Paracelsus

Paracelsus was wrong, of course, but as a thoroughgoing
Christian (at least so he claimed and wisely in those days) he
betrayed in the sentence I have quoted a uniquely Christian
bias. The Christian or, understood in the proper meaning of
the word, Catholic church is a very powerful spiritual
organization. Some Catholic priests I have met are truly holy;
some of the laity in the Christian church are pious in the
original sense of the word, but all too often they betray the
teaching of their Lord by adhering to the letter and not the
spirit of the law. Roman Catholic exorcism is almost
impossible to obtain, despite the fact that most of the Western

Christian churches claim to be the only true path to salvation. And no power on earth, in heaven or in hell, can reconcile the two following statements, which appear in the same pamphlet:

> Exorcism is an act of the Church and not simply of an individual.
>   It should be noted that exorcism can be and has been carried out by any Christian, and even by non-Christians, in the name of Christ.*

As a non-Christian, I acknowledge the tiny nod towards my own right to exist and develop spiritually without benefit of clergy; but as a fairly logical person I feel I must object to this all-too-typical sophistry. Can one exorcise without the church or not? After all, Christ, as the gospels so clearly reveal, was nothing if not an individual. I'm sure he wouldn't mind his name being invoked by anybody in a tight situation, where a human being's peace of mind, heart and soul was at stake. Furthermore, just as Christ opposed the established hierarchy of his own day he certainly would the one that exists today in his name; he would be criticized by the priests of 'his' own religion now, as he was then.

> But the Pharisees said, He casteth out devils through the prince of devils.
> – Matthew 9: 34.

What the hell the prince of devils would be doing bungling his own works is not our concern here. The Pharisees are still around, their name is legion, their argument is now called double-think, and they are doing fairly well in the media of politics and religion. In what one may call Organizational Christianity, the Pharisees are ignoring the problem of exorcism with the supreme air-conditioned calm that the government shows when it ignores inflation. There are cases of possession which have resulted in death, simply because the church turned its head and refused to notice until it was too

* *Exorcism,* op. cit., p. 21.

late. At the other end of the scale there are the Christian Radical Exorcists, who charge in with bell, book and candle to cure a case of tonsillitis. These are the ego-freaks, and they are truly dangerous; though neither the Organizational Christian nor the Christian Radical Exorcist make for very desirable company. What is needed in a case of suspected possession is a rational, trained exorcist who is or is in touch with a trained medic and a psychiatrist. The Roman church has, in its dealings with exorcism and with baptism which is a form of exorcism, often behaved like a spiritual blackmailer. This is much to the discredit of a great spiritual body. But the evidence is overwhelming.

> Then saith he unto his disciples, The harvest truly *is* plenteous, but the labourers are few.
>
> — Matthew 9: 37.

The truly evil — and I mean that word — side of Christianity and Christian exorcism is its utter lack of Christ's own goodwill. We have here an interesting Biblical example:

> But Elymas the sorcerer (for so is his name by interpretation) withstood them, seeking to turn away the deputy from the faith.
> Then Saul (who also is called Paul) filled with the Holy Ghost, set his eyes on him.
> And said, O full of all subtilty and mischief, thou child of the devil, thou enemy of all righteousness, wilt thou not cease to pervert the right ways of the Lord?
> And now behold, the hand of the Lord is upon thee, and thou shalt be blind, not seeing the sun for a season. And immediately there fell on him a mist and a darkness; and he went about seeking some to lead him by the hand.
>
> — The Acts 13: 8-11.

As neat a bit of Black Magic as ever I read of, and performed by the apostle Saul a.k.a. Paul, while spreading the doctrine of love and peace as he learned it from the teachings of Our Lord Jesus Christ. It has been pointed out elsewhere

22

that before his conversion Saul/Paul's favourite pastime was massacring Christians, and that even his conversion didn't change his personal habits much. Just the persuasion of his victims. I have never ceased to be amused by the black humour of the circumstances of Paul's execution. Having been arrested, he was about to be released when he appealed as a Roman citizen (*Civis Romanus sum*) to be sent to Caesar for judgement; an action which proved unwise as he was subsequently beheaded. Not crucified like his Master, you understand. After all, he was a Roman citizen, not a hippie Jew who talked about love all the time.

Incidentally, Father Crehan, SJ, has described this little bit of dirty work on Elymas as an 'exorcism'. The Bible leaves one a little unclear about the facts of the case, but given what it does tell us, well . . . by their fruits you shall know them.

Christ was himself a man of most unpredictable temper, one minute healing a case of leprosy, and the next blasting a figtree. Presumably the leper may have done something in his life to deserve some karmic form of punishment, but it takes a real temper to get mad at a figtree. Often enough, his anger took off in the direction of his apostles, who seem sometimes to be incredibly dense and undeveloped spiritually ('O ye of little faith . . .'). He did, however, hand over to them the power of exorcism:

> And when he had called unto him his twelve disciples, he gave them power over unclean spirits, to cast them out, and to heal all manner of sickness and all manner of disease.
>
> – Matthew 10: 1.

Not that they didn't boob it occasionally, as the *Acts of the Apostles* clearly and sometimes humorously shows. There is a marvellous incident in which St Paul, who was not of course given the power directly by the living Christ, was preaching to a number of people. Apparently he went on a bit, because one of the faithful fell sound asleep while sitting against a window ledge, tumbled over backwards out the window and almost broke his neck. Paul rushed out and healed him, which seems only fair.

23

The Catholic church's claim to the power of exorcism, which it most emphatically does possess, is based on the apostolic succession starting with St Peter and, according to church claims, passing directly from him to the current pontiff. It doesn't seem to matter much to the Vatican that some of these successors can be historically proven never to have existed. The power of the faith of successive generations of human beings is what counts. 'Saint' Christopher may never have walked the earth or trodden water, but many churches still exist in his name; the name is still potent because people believe in it. The church does have the power of exorcism, perhaps for the same reason. But it is that power that concerns us, not the whys and wherefores. Therefore, let us get on to the rudiments of Christian exorcism, ignoring the shortcomings of a great organization. To discuss the spiritual nature of Christian exorcism, a subject one rarely hears about these days, I shall begin, as many Christians seem to have failed to, with Christ.

Exorcism was, of course, nothing new when Christ was born. Neither were demons. He was himself tempted in the desert but, emerging the master of himself, he showed remarkable power over the negative powers of the universe.

> And his fame went throughout all Syria: and they brought unto him all sick people that were taken with divers diseases and torments, and those which were possessed with devils . . . and he healed them.
>
> – Matthew 4: 24.

Certain Biblical incidents show that, at the beginning of his career at least, Christ was anxious to keep his healing powers a secret, however willing he was to use them when necessary. As Bernard Shaw has pointed out, it was only towards the end of his three-year preaching period that he began to announce himself as the Messiah. But by invoking the power of the Father, he amassed a record of genuine healing and of exorcisms not since surpassed. One is right to call him Master. He must have failed once in a while but the gospels do not report it.

He is a lonely figure, this Gallilean who once remarked that

24

the fox and the bird had a place to rest their heads but the Son of Man had nowhere to call home. One sees him very much as he is portrayed in the motion picture version of *Jesus Christ, Superstar,* wandering off into the endless desert while his disciples and girl friend call him back – hopelessly, because they seek to impose conditions upon him that he knows are impossible if he is to succeed in his mission. Christ, healer and exorcist, did not always like what he had to do. A true exorcist does not expect to live long: the permutations of what may go unexpectedly wrong at any moment are endless and even momentary cowardice might prove fatal. (A war hero once remarked that the difference between a hero and a coward is a fraction of a second.) So we find in the gospels a man of tremendous spiritual resources who could go for over a month without food. Quite understandably, he found himself a little alone in the presence of his inferiors.

> When the unclean spirit is gone out of a man, he walketh through dry places, seeking rest, and findeth none.
> Then he saith, I will return into my house from whence I came out; and when he is come, he findeth it empty, swept, and garnished.
> – Matthew 12: 43-44.

Not that Christ was not powerful enough to exorcise himself; indeed he was. But out there in the desert he must have felt that state of despair (as did St Anthony) which St John of the Cross called the dark night of the soul. To attain this state of heightened spirituality one must surrender everything, even the will to surrender. To paraphrase a famous modern poet, the real deserts have no tradition. They are not Wiccan, they are not High or Low Church of England, they are not Roman Catholic, and they are not Buddhist. 'The Kingdom of God is within you' and, if you cannot find it there, you will never find it in incense or Lourdes water or talismans or by filling up the collection plate.

The significance of Christ's action in driving out the money changers from the Temple is obvious here. I once knew a nun who sincerely believed that the reason for Christ so acting was

25

that the money changers were short-changing all the foreigners. In fact, money changers and Temples do not go very well together. If Christ could see the nuns selling ugly religious items at the Vatican he would probably feel the same anger. One does not *buy* spiritual power, and that includes the power to exorcise.

> Then certain of the vagabond Jews, exorcists, took upon them to call over them which had evil spirits the name of the lord Jesus, saying, we adjure you by Jesus whom Paul preacheth.
> And there were seven sons of *one* Sceva, a Jew and chief of the priests, which did so.
> And the evil spirit answered and said, Jesus I know, and Paul I know, but who are ye?
> And the man in whom the evil spirit was leaped on them, and overcame them, and prevailed against them, so that they fled out of that house naked and wounded.
> — The Acts 19: 13-16.

I've often wondered about that naked bit, but no matter. The thing to remember is that formulae, Witch, Christian or Mantric, are useless if the whole mind, body and spirit of the exorcist are not pure and totally dedicated to his work. The apostles themselves discovered this to their sorrow.

In Christian exorcism as it exists today, all too often the priest is not spiritually developed enough to carry out even the rudiments of the discipline required. He has, presumably, been ordained an exorcist, but his knowledge of the subject is scanty and generally academic. If faced with a real demon any normal person in his right mind would turn tail and run, but a priest of Christ should have power over demons – anyway, that's the claim.

I think we must face the fact that the power of exorcism is often a *personal* power; at least insofar as the individual is capable of allowing supernormal forces to work through him in order to correct 'a distortion of right orderliness'. Humility is required as well as power – or, shall we say, there is power to be gained through true humility. At the Last Supper Christ washed the feet of his apostles, men of far less power than he, men in fact far less capable of humility.

In contrast to this *personal* element, Christian exorcism (normally based on the ritual of the *Rituale Romanum*) is considered to be effective *ex opere operato,* that is, by virtue of the ritual itself, rather than *ex opere operando,* by the trained will and dedication of the operator. Unfortunately, even though the Roman Ritual is very powerful, this does not always work. I have seen a young priest attempt an exorcism (he had never done one before) on a house, and although one could feel the power being raised at first, it suddenly flopped like a failed omelet. The house has been plagued with ill luck ever since. He simply did not have the power to exorcise, though he has a 'licence' to perform exorcism. The Christian church has got to acknowledge the role of personal power in exorcism. Thanks to the efforts of the now retired Bishop of Exeter, it is, in some measure, facing this issue.

Christian exorcisms are performed, generally speaking, in four situations: upon those seeking baptism; upon unblessed objects to be used for ritual or accursed objects; upon places, such as haunted houses; and upon persons who are deemed to be possessed.

The blessing of persons seeking baptism involves a renunciation of the devil and all his works. In the middle ages, as now, this renunciation was pronounced on behalf of the six-to-ten-day-old infant by his godparents. Further, the child is committed to Christianity forever – and few and far between are the babies who are in a position to dispute the matter. Christ did, if we give or take ten years; after going through the normal Jewish rites of purification as a baby, he returned, still a child, to the Temple, to confound his elders and 'betters' with the logic of his arguments against them; and this at a very tender age and without the consent of his parents. He received baptism of his own free will and as a fully grown man at the hands of his cousin, John the Baptist. He did in fact *seek* baptism, not have it lumbered upon him at infancy. John at first was hesitant to baptize Jesus, saying that he, John, was not worthy; probably this was true, but again we see Christ, the future exorcist, showing true humility. The Christian seeking baptism, the catechumen, must take certain vows of which he should be made totally aware. Infants should of course be exorcised of any evil influence; in other words, blessed, absolved of any possible karmic 'distortion of right orderliness'.

No forms of exorcism appear in the *Apostolic Tradition* of the Christian Hippolytus; the early Christian church seems to have regarded all sacraments as a form of positive exorcism, as a purification, and then an enrichment of life. In the Roman Mass, communion comes after an elaborate rite of exorcism performed at the foot of the altar, followed by a blessing, then an invocation, then consecration.

In the passage I have quoted from Matthew 10: 1, in which Jesus gave his apostles power 'over unclean spirits . . . and [the power to] heal all manner of sickness', there seems to be little distinction in the mind of the author between physical and psychic illness. It is curious for the modern mind to think of penicillin as a sort of exorcism, but it would not have seemed odd to Jesus's contemporaries. The same applies to Christian baptism as to giving out aspirins. One does not give an open bottle of aspirin to a child to play with, though on medical advice may feed a half-tablet to a baby. Similarly infants are in no position to make or break vows, but they do need taking care of. They should be exorcised by a proper cleric, but not spoken for as to which path they will choose for spiritual development. The adult seeking baptism or exorcism has had time to think things over, to realize his spiritual needs, and if necessary to consult an exorcist. He has had a chance to give the devil his due.

The exorcism and blessing of objects is quite commonly practised in the Christian church, and the ritual of asperging is well-known to anyone who has asked for the blessing of an object by a priest. Sometimes the practice is merely superstitious, sometimes downright ridiculous. I once had the dubious spiritual experience of seeing a priest bless a two-tone Buick. This tradition dates back to pagan times, however; and the blessing of a fleet of fishing vessels on the appropriate Christian feast day is very moving and no doubt efficacious. Christian objects to be used in the various rituals are given a very thorough going-over and do have a definite spiritual radiance of which any psychic in their presence is immediately aware.

One of the first psychics I ever met, a woman nearly blind but amazingly perceptive who put me in touch with my dead father, had a curious experience once with a crucifix. She had bought it in Spain, but every time she wore it the cross turned face backwards on her chest. It happened that the maker of these crosses was an extremely evil man who put a curse on every one he made. She instructed her husband to take the cross and throw it far out into a lake near their house, thereby nullifying the evil influence and making sure (one hopes) that the cross never came into anyone else's possession. Competent Christian exorcists can cleanse and bless such objects. Should you have such a suspicious medallion that you wear or keep at home, you would be well advised to consult someone who can do something about it.

Christian places of worship are traditionally exorcised and consecrated. If they have been violated, by Satanists for example, they must be re-consecrated. But far more interesting, I suppose, are cases in which particular sites have been 'possessed' or otherwise disturbed by discarnate human beings, spirits, or psychic forces such as poltergeists, which are often caused by people living about the premises. A house or room in which murder has been committed, for example, may well be 'haunted' by the victim or even the murderer returning, albeit a little late, to the scene of the crime. I know of one such house in America in which a young man committed suicide. He returns occasionally to hang himself again, much to the discomfort of anyone who happens to be sleeping in the room at the time. Another house in California has one room which is most uncomfortable to enter; it is the dining room, in which the culmination of a most unhappy marriage resulted in an act of violence. The actress Elke Sommer experienced psychic disturbance in a house which tended to set itself on fire.

England has been described as the most haunted country in the world and it certainly deserves the title. Just around the corner from where my wife and I used to live near the Kilburn

High Road in London, there is a discarnate spirit who makes himself known in various ways, one of which is running down the stairs in the middle of the night. ('I don't mind him,' one tenant told us, 'but he always *jumps* the last two stairs.') This entity seems to be entirely benevolent. In fact, in times of stress, he has been known to comfort some of the people living in the house. In other instances hauntings are merely amusing, as in the case of a departed old man who kept returning to a house to try to find his false teeth. When they were placed where he could find them, they apparently disappeared and the disturbances ceased. But some hauntings are not so funny. Places, like people, can absorb evil vibrations, and give them off again. Belsen concentration camp had to be exorcised, and there are many sites which are in similar if not so drastic need of a good psychic cleansing. The Christian rite of exorcism can be, if performed by a competent exorcist, most effective in such cases.

If the place to be exorcised is a residence, the exorcist begins by gathering all who live in the house in the room where most disturbance is felt, or the room which is most frequented by everyone. Prayers are recited; then exorcism is pronounced. The formula of exorcism used by Neil-Smith would be appropriate (p. 123), or this one, given in the pamphlet *Exorcism* (p. 32):

> God, the Son of God, who by death destroyed death, and overcame him who had the power of death.
> Beat down Satan quickly.
> Deliver this place (room, house, church) from all evil spirits; all vain imaginations, projections and phantasms; and all deceits of the evil one; and bid them harm no one but depart to the place appointed to them, there to remain forever.
> God, incarnate God, who came to give peace, bring peace.

The exorcist asperges the room with holy water then proceeds to go round the building, accompanied by his assistants, repeating the process in every room or wherever the disturbance seems to have focused. Afterwards the house is blessed in similar fashion as are all its inhabitants.

The Christian form of exorcism of persons has been fairly accurately depicted in the motion picture, *The Exorcist*. Having seen the movie several times before its release and given an interview on it, I became convinced that what was causing my fellow viewers so much distress – several persons rushed out of the theatre, and chain-smoking was so rampant that the air was every bit as infernal as the subject of the picture – I became convinced that what was truly disturbing was that the audience sensed that what they were seeing was true. This was not just another horror picture, but a semi-documentary of an actual case of possession, and those who sensed this were affected in the extreme.

Christian exorcism is not, as we have seen, an office limited to ordained priests. But under normal conditions it is performed by at least two priests, one of whom is the exorcist proper and the other serving as an assistant. Prayer, fasting and communion are recommended before undertaking the exorcism. Often there is very little time for this, so the exorcist should himself already be by lifetime habit 'in a state of recollection and confident of our Lord's victory over evil in general and in the situation confronting him'.*

The exorcism should preferably take place in a church, not in the presence of any person who may prove hostile, consciously or otherwise, but along with various sympathetic and spiritually attuned people to restrain the patient in case of violence† and doctors (a GP and a psychiatrist) if possible.

The actual form of the exorcism may vary. (However, a passage from the Roman Catholic Ritual, *Rituale Romanum,* is given further on in this book.) When the exorcism is completed, sacraments and a blessing may be administered.

In general, although the rites of Christian exorcism are very powerful, ritual formulae alone do not an exorcism make. Far

* *Exorcism*, p. 35.
† Kurt Koch, the German exorcist, has described in his book *Demonology, Past and Present* (Michigan: Kregel Publications, 1973) how a normally frail young man who was possessed needed nine strong men to restrain him during the process of being exorcised.

31

too few Christian clergymen are trained in the field – despite the fact that the need of Christians for spiritual leaders, including exorcists, is becoming cryingly more apparent. The problem is compounded by the church's insanely bureaucratic structure, which makes exorcism virtually impossible to obtain. This attitude is all the more difficult to understand when one considers that exorcism was not only a common practice of Christ and his apostles, but is a prescribed rite of the church. The church has only itself to blame if, having failed its flock, the sheep tend to wander off in droves.

2 Social exorcism: from the Middle Ages to the 'Age of Reason'

Between roughly the eleventh and the eighteenth centuries, an estimated nine million heretics and 'Witches' – it now seems doubtful that even a majority of these 'Witches' were actually members of the Craft – were executed by the civil authorities acting in League with the Roman Catholic church. This might be regarded as sheer mass hysteria, but the operations were just as well-planned and financed as Hitler's extermination of the Jews. (It is interesting to note, by the way, that Germany was the centre of the Witch persecutions, and the burning of Witches in Germany seems to have attracted the largest and most enthusiastic crowds. When Hitler decided that the 'final solution' to the Jewish problem was to kill six million Jews, he had a historical precedent.) The actions of the church, the lynch mobs and the civil authorities trying to rid the community of devil worshippers and Witches – the two soon became erroneously synonymous – were in a sense a form of misguided social exorcism. The same might be said of Hitler's actions concerning the Jews. It is a truism that the gods of one religion become the devils of the succeeding religion, and 'Begone Satan!' may be easily translated into 'Begone Witches!' or 'Begone Jews!' In the case of the Jews, Satan took on a distinctly economic-evil-all-caused-by-these-devils appearance. In the case of the Witches and such heretical groups as the Cathars and the Knights Templar, it was only necessary to identify these sects with Satan to instigate one of the most hideous and prolonged blood baths in human history.

What, in fact, are the origins of 'Satan'? Richard Cavendish* has done a superb job of compiling the literary

* *The Black Arts* (Routledge & Kegan Paul), pp. 283-99.

33

sources, Biblical and otherwise, of this enthralling character whose charisma is such that Milton inadvertently made him the scene-stealer of *Paradise Lost*. Etymologically, *satan* means only 'one who bars the way', or 'opponent'. Originally there were many satans, not all of them spirits; one might regard them, using modern terms, as simply enemies or competitors. But God and Satan were not, originally, enemies. Satan, or satans, performed much the same role as that of the Devil's Advocate in the church's procedure of canonization: they stood before God and accused the righteous and evil alike.

In the Book of Job, we find a presumably individual 'opponent' debating with God as to whether Job honours the Lord because he's happy and prosperous or because he truly loves the Lord. This conversation, conducted on as friendly a level as one might expect to hear over a chess game, indicates that Yehovah and Satan are at least on civil terms, though they might differ over a point or two. If Job really loves the Lord, however, he seems by any interpretation to have made a fair-weather friend (especially as, in this case, the friend makes the weather). Job is afflicted as no man ever was. He does not give up on Yehovah, but he does challenge him as to his reasons for permitting the satan to carry on like this. God responds by coming down and bawling him out for asking. We are faced here with the theological problem of the existence of evil. The upshot is that God restores Job's health and gives him another family so he can start all over again. But all one can say about God's actions is: Some joke.

The satan is clearly, however, still a servant of God as we find him in Job. Not until the church fathers decided to interpret a certain passage in Isaiah as indicative of the fall of a satan through rebellion against God do we get any indication of what is to come.

> How art thou fallen from heaven, O Lucifer, son of the morning! How art thou cut down to the ground which did weaken the nations! For thou hast said in thine heart, I will ascend into heaven, I will exalt my throne above the stars of God: I will sit also in the mount of the congregation upon the sides of the north: I will ascend

above the height of the clouds; I will be like the most High. Yet thou shalt be brought down to hell, to the sides of the pit.

– Isaiah 14: 12-15.

Interpreted on a more mundane level, this could easily be taken as a prediction by Isaiah, who was a bit of a grumpy sort, that the king of Babylon will be defeated. But if we equate Satan, who is an amalgamation of the older satans, with Lucifer, the 'light bearer', we have the Christian basis for explaining the endless battle between God and the Devil, right and wrong, good and evil. Satan in his pride defied Yehovah and was cast down to 'hell, to the sides of the pit'. In order to test the mettle of men, God allows him to go wandering up and down the earth, tempting even the righteous and generally raising hell. The problem of the existence of evil has been glossed over, if not solved exactly. The church is on God's side. Anyone not on the church's side is on the side of the Devil. Hence the Devil, from the Greek meaning 'little god', is to be renounced *along with all his works*. This included those nine million executed people, many of whom undoubtedly did not even understand the charges levelled against them.

The details of the execution of so-called heretics and Witches and the methods by which they were 'tried' are fairly well known, but never fail to inspire horror at the human potential for cruelty. They have their place in a book on exorcism because they were or seemed to be in the eyes of the Inquisition an exorcism of the community: the cattle, the crops, and the church as a living organism composed of the faithful. Suspected Witches were stripped naked, all of their bodily hair shaven, and they were continually pricked with needles. That experience was excruciating and finally numbing, so that when the examiner found what he was looking for, a place on the body that did not respond to pain (thus proving the accused a Witch), the rest was easy. The accused was 'watched', having to remain motionless or run backwards and forwards naked across his cell for days on end. If so much as a fly got into the cell during this time, it was a

35

clear sign that the prisoner possessed a 'familiar' who had come to visit him. Often other tortures were imposed: one of the most sadistic was the rack, or tying the prisoner's hands behind his back and raising him, pulley-style, high into the air by tossing the rope across a beam. The usual paraphernalia of the time, such as thumb screws and devices to shatter the bones of the feet, were, according to the transcripts that exist of the trials, applied *ad lib*. One of the most idiotic means of 'testing' whether a person was a Witch or not was to bind him right wrist to left ankle and vice versa, then toss him into a pond to see if he sank or not. If he sank he was innocent but usually dead from drowning. If he floated he was guilty, fished out and burned. The human body tends to float naturally on water, as anyone will know who has tried to 'sink' into a deep, hot bath. I have often pictured myself in this position of being 'tried', not out of paranoia but because I like diving, and have come to the conclusion that I would probably, because of the way in which I was bound, find myself floating face-down in the water drowning while my fellow townsmen were cheering merrily away; if, by a superhuman effort I could manage to swing over on to my back, I would be hauled out, dried off and burned at the stake. A pretty young English Witch once told me, proudly and ingenuously, that although Witches were burned in Scotland, no such thing ever took place in England. Perhaps not officially. Witches were not burned but heretics were, and Witches were heretics.

It was during the period of church persecutions that Witches became confused with Satanists. In the popular press, therefore in the mind of the public, this confusion still remains, dating back some hundreds of years. In fact, although I am acquainted with some Luciferians, I have never to my knowledge met a Witch who is also a Satanist, though there is no reason why a Satanist should not be a Witch. (One Anglican minister whom I know is also a Witch.) But true Satanism has nothing doctrinally or in practice to do with Witchcraft, nor do Witches have anything to do with the Black Mass, at least not while performing as Witches. The deceased Dr Gerald Gardner, who became a Witch high priest and the founder of Gardnerian Witchcraft, has the following to say about his initiation:

> One of the first questions I had asked witches as soon as I had got 'inside' was, 'What about the Black Mass?' They all said, 'We don't know how to perform it, and if we did, what would be the point of doing so?' They also said, 'You know what happens at our meetings . . . There is no time or place for any nonsense of "Black Masses" and anyhow, why should we want to do one?' *

Gardner explains further:

> I think this is just common sense. To a Roman Catholic who believes in Transubstantiation, that is, that the bread and wine of the Mass are literally changed into the flesh and blood of Christ, a ceremonial insult to the Host would be the most awful blasphemy: *but witches do not believe this, so it would simply be absurd to them to try to insult a piece of bread.* *

Even professed Satanists such as Anton Szandor LaVey, the 'Black Pope' of San Francisco's First Church of Satan, regard the Black Mass as something of an absurdity.

> Any ceremony considered a black mass must effectively shock and outrage, as this seems to be the measure of its success. In the Middle Ages, blaspheming the holy church was shocking. Now, however, the Church does not present the awesome image it did during the inquisition . . .
>
> A black mass, today, would consist of the blaspheming of such 'sacred' topics as Eastern mysticism, psychiatry, the psychedelic movement, ultra-liberalism, etc. Patriotism would be championed, drugs and their gurus would be defiled, and the decadence of ecclesiastical theologies might even be given a Satanic boost.†

* Dr G. B. Gardner, *The Meaning of Witchcraft,* The Aquarian Press, 1959, p. 13.
† Anton Szandor Lavey, *The Satanic Bible,* Avon Publishers, p. 101.

This is not to imply that the Black Mass did not and does not exist: it did and it does. I have seen a copy of the ritual. But it never had anything to do with Witchcraft, not even in medieval times, except insofar as a practising Witch may also have been a practising Satanist. A very great percentage of the victims who 'confessed' to having signed a pact with Satan, having been made 'an offer which they could not refuse' by their inquisitors, later protested their innocence and attested that they had only agreed to confess because of the pain of the torture. Naturally – or unnaturally – this was regarded by the judges as a sign that they were backsliding, so the tortures were resumed, 'for the sake of their souls'. The pathology of such social exorcists as Father James Sprenger and Father Henry Krämer, authors of the *Malleus Maleficarum,* a notorious textbook on how to 'deal' with Witches widely circulated during medieval times, must have been interesting. 'In charity they condemned.' *

The torturing and executions lasted well into the eighteenth century, though one normally thinks of them as exclusively medieval. (In fact, the British law against practising Witchcraft was only repealed in the 1950s.) The 'Age of Reason' continued to fear the Unknown; men like Newton, upon whose discoveries so much of modern physics has been based, practised astrology. A sermon to be preached against the 'detestable' practices of Witchcraft, sorcery and divination in general was still being preached annually on Lady Day at Queens' College, Cambridge, in 1718.[†] I have never seen the phrase 'social exorcism' used before, but if we regard exorcism in general as the binding of evil forces, this is certainly what the civil and clerical authorites during that period at least pretended to have in mind. In succeeding centuries with the decline of established religion, the process of what used generally to be called exorcism became, on the personal level, psychiatric or the concern of the GP, and on the social level, political. Both have failed to fulfil a fundamentally spiritual need.

Françoise Strachan made an excellent remark when she

* Pennethorne Hughes, *Witchcraft,* Penguin, p. 180.
† Hughes, op. cit., p. 180.

observed that 'one builds up a fear of evil, but unless one acquires an understanding of evil instead of a wrong sort of fear, true contact with God is not possible'.* This fear is precisely one of the things which motivated the Witch hunters; they are still very much with us, practising their own form of social exorcism. Potentially another social exorcist is the sort of 'rational' person who panics at the thought that anything can exist which cannot be immediately identified, defined and categorized. How does this sort pluck up the courage to switch on a television, since no one has satisfactorily been able to identify, define or categorize electricity? In a position of authority (which he may well attain, since he puts on such a good show of understanding everything) he too will become a social exorcist, sacking the first delivery boy who shows up on the job with long hair. In trying to rid themselves of a devil they themselves created, the social exorcists of the traditional Western church have ignored what the Spanish philospher Unamuno knew very well: We die of cold, but not of darkness.

* *Casting out the Devils*, p. 105.

3 Exorcism in other orthodox religions

The rite of exorcism is pre-Christian and exists entirely independently of Christianity. Father Crehan* has pointed out that in Acts 19: 13 we find St Paul arriving at Ephesus to find Jewish exorcists, who presumably had had no contact with Christianity, already performing exorcisms. After Paul's arrival they added the name of Jesus to their list of Names of Power for banishing evil spirits.

If the bias of this book has so far been towards Christian and contemporary pagan attitudes towards exorcism, that is because the majority of readers will link up the term 'exorcism' with either one or the other. However, the Greek and Russian Orthodox churches have their own forms of Christian exorcism, which seem very powerful indeed. Such religions as Buddhism and Judaism are turning away from the concept of demonology and going very much the way of modern psychiatry. In this they are not unlike, surprisingly, Islam. The Buddhist is not so much interested in expelling demons as in creating an auric healthiness which no evil influence can harm. Modern Judaism has lost so much of its spirituality that the *Dybbuk,* or devil, has been reduced in contemporary Jewish literature to a dramatic source for plays and short stories. Servants of Allah seem to regard demonic possession of the faithful as impossible if the Koran is obeyed to the letter. I wish they were right.

* *Exorcism,* op. cit. .

4 'Pagan' exorcism

In primitive societies even today the Witch Doctor is regarded as both healer and exorcist. Indeed, as with early Christianity, we find that these two functions are indistinguishable. Any healing is a form of exorcism, insofar as it dispels an evil force or, more precisely, restores a condition of right orderliness.

Though literary sources are rare, exorcism dates back many years before Christianity. Hebraic and Christian forms of exorcism are derived from Egyptian rituals, one of which I shall shortly give. Christianity did not invent Satan, it merely changed his name. *Eblis, Maskim, Typhon, Ahriman, Beelzebub, Astaroth, Astarte, Moloch, Asmodeus, Dev, Dybbuk, Set* are all words personifying the Prince of Darkness as the ruler of the negative forces of the universe, in his function in a particular instance. Demons are invoked for different purposes, and any one of them can be the Devil. In order to overcome *Set*, Lord of Darkness, for example, an exorcist of Egypt during the Eleventh Dynasty would have stood facing the sun at midday, raising his arms in greeting to it, invoking *Ra:*

> Hail unto thee who art our Ahathoor in thy triumphing, by whose power all things have life.
>
> Let thy force, which is in the winds of the air, and in the earth, and in the seed of the grain below the earth, in the source of all rivers and in the coming forth of leaves, and in the animals with which they share their strength, and in all men who live by their divinity,
>
> Let thy force give to this son [daughter] of thy son [daughter] until the thousandth generation, who am of men called [*Magical name*] thy strength; by which I may bring forth into thy light this spirit you have not yet

41

named.

Let there be your life in my fingers, so that I may make live your sign to live upon his forehead, so that the shadow is lifted and fear is a stranger to him.

Let thy seal be upon his mouth, so that no echo of the underworld cometh forth from between his lips.

Let thy seal be upon his ears, so that the whispers of the unclean cannot enter herein.

Let thy seal be upon his eyes, so that they can see beyond the shadows of the benificence of thy midday sun.

Let thy seal be upon his nostrils, so that myrrh, aloes, cedar and alum are not so eager to them as is the incense of thy temple.

Let thy seal be upon his head and the palms of his hands, upon his breasts and upon his navel, upon the division of his loins, upon his knees and upon the soles of his feet.

So that in his going forth and in his waking, in his nurture and in his breathing,

In his seeing and in his hearing,

In his eating and in his planting,*

In his going forth and returning,

He may know that he is no longer a nameless one, but a child of a child to the ten thousandth generation of the Lord of the Midday Sky.

After reciting this, the exorcist would touch the disturbed person on his head, ears, mouth and nostrils. Then, making the sign of *Ra* on his breast, navel, knees, phallus and the soles of his feet, he would issue the following ultimatum:

Set, I challenge you to come forth from your caverns to do battle against the name of Ahathoor, for this child *N*†
who is now newborn out of the womb of the earth under

* For convenience I have given the ritual as if the disturbed person were male; obviously 'her' would be substituted for 'him' wherever appropriate, and instead of 'planting' the priest would say 'conceiving'.

† Again, the 'Magical' name, that name one gives only to friends.

the sun, pledged by Ahathoor to our company. Begone, *Set!* Begone, *Sekmet* and all your shadowy host! Or see for yourself that this link is broken! Come forth to my challenge in the name of Ahathoor!

This ritual is still being used today. It was sent to me by an adept who appended: 'I sincerely hope this is of some use to you. If not for the book then maybe you can use it practically if you should ever need it. It works: I know.' She added a night invocation to be used every evening as a form of psychic protection from the forces of *Set*. Facing north, one says:

Hail unto Thee who art Kephra in Thy Hiding,
Even unto Thee who art Kephra in Thy Silence,
Who travellest over the heavens in Thy bark at the midnight hour of the sun.
Hail unto Thee from the abodes of evening.

Anyone familiar with the Witches' Ritual of the Openings (given on p. 87) will recognize similarities between the ancient ritual just quoted and one practised today by modern Witches. In fact non-Christian exorcism is still very much alive and breathing, and often succeeds where Christian exorcism has failed.

The difference between exorcisms performed by a priest and those performed by a professed magician is that the priest relies on his invocations to God to do the work, whereas the magician commands, often drawing the alien spirit into himself and then, as one excellent magician told me, 'digests it', distilling it back into its proper place. Such an operation is obviously risky. It is not always successful. Even if it is successful in part, the exorcist, if inexperienced, may find himself lumbered with a most unwelcome psychic guest.

One increasingly common form of exorcism, now that magical equipment is relatively easy to obtain, is by means of a consecrated object known as the Trident of Paracelsus. This is a spear, a magical sword, whereby the offending entity is jabbed out of a person's aura.

The whole of the person's aura and its surroundings should be punctured with short stabs, and if the sharp points contact an entity, the trident acts as a lightning-arrester, which discharges accumulated magnetism and so presents a thunderbolt. The stabs should apparently be quite numerous as some of the entities can be quite small and liable to escape, but there are also large entities which may need a number of stabs before they are completely eradicated. It is said that the demons cannot see the exorcist, but are able to see the magnetized trident. They are able to see the points of the trident, which to them are apparently similar to radiant luminous needle-points.

Françoise Strachan, whom I have just quoted,* rarely makes a mistake in her research but in fact she is wrong in assuming that this trident was designed to dispel any harmful entities. But this is a moot point at best, since the thing seems to work all right as a ritual tool for exorcism.

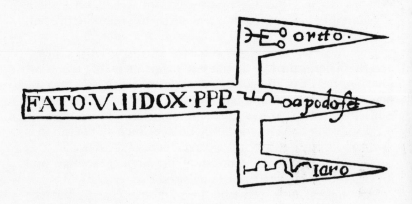

* *Casting out the Devils*, p. 102.

It may seem a little incongruous to the more orthodox but Satanists, too, perform exorcisms. Perhaps, this sounds like the pot calling the kettle black magic, but a truly moral Satanist (yes, there are such creatures) deplores psychic vampirism as thoroughly as does the White Witch. In what he calls the 'Invocation Employed towards the Conjuration of Compassion', Anton Szandor Levey unwittingly – or perhaps fully consciously – parrots the Bible, substituting the name of Satan for Yehovah. The invocation is to be recited for one who is oppressed, psychically or otherwise.

> Restore him to power, to joy, to unending dominion over the reverses that have beset him.
>
> Build around and within him the exultant radiance that will herald his emergence from the stagnant morass which engulfs him.
>
> As Satan reigns so shall his own whose name is as this sound: N is the vessel whose flesh is as the earth; life everlasting, world without end!*

Substitute 'God' for 'Satan' and that passage would not at all have displeased the authors of the Psalms.

Talismans, too, are often effective against psychic attack. But the danger here is that attachment to an object can often result in fetishism and the loss of the object can bring about a trauma horrible beyond the dreams of the most virulent psychic attacker. I once presented a friend with an Egyptian talisman which had been carved out in wood. It was copied from a book of Solomon and is a symbol of protection. One night it disappeared, and she telephoned me in a frenzy. She had turned the apartment upside down but it was nowhere to be found. Several days later it simply appeared under her dresser, in a place which she had thoroughly searched. I am at a loss to explain its disappearance and recovery, but the incident does show that 'lucky charms' should be very well taken care of or not used at all. The crucifix, the saint's relic and the Witch's pentacle are all meaningless if the living, vital

---

* *The Satanic Bible*, p. 152.

person who possesses them does not, himself, will himself well.

Another fundamental difference between Christian and non-Christian exorcism is that the Catholic priest, working according to the *Rituale Romanum,* begins first by invoking the power of God and then proceeds immediately to threaten whatever entity is afflicting the disturbed person. He commands it and generally bosses it about before he has determined whether a show of force is preferable to a little goodwill and reason. This latter approach has been ridiculed as the 'tea and sympathy' approach to exorcism, yet it can and has worked without risking the trauma of a fullscale, ritual exorcism. Non-Christian exorcists have a distinct advantage in that they do not despise 'Satan': in some ways, they feel, he's just got a bad press. They see no harm in conjuring the angel Lucifer, who usually appears not as a horned monstrosity but as a beautiful, radiant boy. Everything in the universe has its place, and the non-Christian exorcist has as much respect for the right of 'demons' to exist as for 'angels'. It is only a question of assuring that everything *is* in its proper place. And as Bertrand Russell remarked once, only a very cruel person could have invented Hell.

PART III

Conversations with modern exorcists

'Do I contradict myself? . . .'

– Walt Whitman

1   The Reverend Christopher Neil-Smith

'Some exorcists are only able to perform about one exorcism in six months, and others do them several times a day. This again depends very greatly on the strength of the physical, mental, and psychic make-up of the exorcist.'

– Francoise Strachan

'I've performed, I suppose . . . a thousand exorcisms in the past year.'   – Christopher Neil-Smith

A Witch priestess once remarked to me that when Christopher

Neil-Smith was ordained an Anglican minister the world lost a highly promising Witch. I agree but am not sure that I'm unecumenical enough to regret the loss. Many Witches, as well as Buddhists, atheists, Roman Catholics and Anglicans, have reason to thank him for his help. His help is rarely refused. He has been criticized by many persons in the occult world, sometimes out of jealousy, but in the long time I have known him he has never failed to take on cases of obsession or possession which have had 'orthodox' religious or medical practitioners fleeing from the room in terror. He is one of the world's most respected exorcists, and deservedly so.

But were it not for the Roman collar, I would at first glance take Christopher Neil-Smith for a Witch, and an adept. I hope he doesn't mind me saying this; he has been most eloquent in his own denunciation of Witchcraft.

> This force [Witchcraft] is not on the same wavelength as power used by Christ. 'Witchcraft' which is sometimes considered to be a 'fertility cult' derives its power from natural forces like the moon (white), or in some of its more sinister forms through 'devil-worship' (black).*

I'm not sure that deriving power from natural forces is necessarily a bad thing, in fact I wonder what the natural forces are there for if not to derive power from them. Or that 'the devil' as popularly understood is a 'natural force'. But Neil-Smith's position is clear: he is an Anglican minister, a priest of Jesus Christ and a very powerful psychic and exorcist. He is the first person I would think of to recommend to anyone with psychic disturbance. It has been my pleasure to have a running conversation with him for years. I use the word 'running' because Neil-Smith thinks, intuits and decides matters usually with uncanny accuracy faster than any man I have ever met.

R. How did you become interested in exorcism?
C. Well I was exorcised myself and through being exorcised I realised the need of such a thing for many other people.

* *The Exorcist And The Possessed*, p. 63.

48

R. You are a very psychic person, you knew that before.

C. Yes, I've always known that I could see things which other people didn't appear to see. There is no doubt that when I interview people I discern certain things about them that they have never been aware of before.

R. Such as? Discern me at the moment.

C. As regarding this particular thing I would say you are clear. At the moment. [*Laughter*]

R. And so you were exorcised. Tell me about an exorcism you yourself performed.

C. Well one of the cases was of a 'Hell's Angel' who had been quite violent, and I was asked to do an exorcism in prison. So I went into the prison with the Captain, and quite frankly when I saw the man he terrified me. I mean, he was 6ft and so on and looked quite ominous. He was quite convinced that there was a force on him which made him do things against his own judgement.

R. He could tell you this? You had a talk with him?

C. Oh, yes. And it was quite clear that he wanted to be released from it. He wasn't just playing a game. It wasn't a stunt. And when I did the exorcism he went right out. Into a complete faint and had to be brought round with Holy Water. And when he was brought round he wandered about the place saying 'It's gone'. When I asked 'What's gone?' he said 'Well, this evil force'. This feeling that he wanted to kill people had disappeared. I think this was definitely an evil spirit.

R. How do you define an 'evil spirit'?

C. Well, I would say that an evil spirit is an entity that intends harm.

R. Which exists outside the person?

C, As I think, yes. But it grips on to a person and makes him do things.

R. Hmm. We'll have to talk about the Taylor case. What is your opinion?

C. I think in some ways he [Taylor] was evil. I mean evil had got hold of him and this is why it had this expression. It is difficult to know exactly *how* that evil got into him. I don't think it got into him through exorcism. I think it was there before and they weren't able to remove it.

R. Want to give me a quick definition of exorcism?

C. Yes. I would say that exorcism is the *driving* away of evil spirits, or the *drawing* away of departed spirits, from a person or a place.

R. Interesting that you use the word *driving*. Isn't it possible that you can coax an evil spirit away? Not by a show of weakness but by a show of understanding?

C. With a departed spirit you can, but I wouldn't say one could coax an evil spirit . . .

R. Not one of those big ones.

C. . . . really intent on one thing and this kind of entity has really got to be commanded. But I think a departed spirit has definitely got to be persuaded, or coaxed away, from a person, by talking to the spirit, if necessary.

R. Do you do this?

C, I have challenged a spirit, yes. And made contact and released it – as I believe you have.

R. Yes. But I wouldn't get in your way if you started driving.

C. Speaking of driving, one of the cases I have dealt with was a man who claimed to have killed someone and he said it was a 'force' that had made him do it. And when I started to do the exorcism the 'force' on him was so great that it threw me some feet away.

R. You were actually levitated and thrown?

C. Yes, and I came to and got up and went back and carried on, and it ultimately cleared.

R. How long were you out?

C. Oh, it was only a split second I suppose.

R. What happened after that?

C. He claimed that this thing cleared. He no longer had this desire.

R. What do you do when you perform an exorcism? Do you use a purple stole, or? . . .

C. Yes, I use a purple stole around my neck. I make the sign of the cross over the person and command, in the case of an evil spirit, command it to depart and go to the place prepared; then I place my hands on the person and there is a tremendous movement through my hands which drives out the evil from the person. But this would not be the case where

50

there is a departed spirit as a person – evil spirits I consider to be *demons* in persons.

R. Do you invoke something to do this?

C. Yes. I would say this was the Holy Spirit, or a holy spirit, coming in, taking over if you like; and that the power in my hands is coming from beyond myself.

R. Why you? Why not anyone in the street?

C. Who can tell? I mean, some people seem to have a particular gift and others haven't. Like musicians, artists or whatever. Some can and others can't.

R. Obviously you regard it as a gift.

C. Yes, I do.

R. And you use it any time you are asked?

C. Well normally speaking I would, yes. Where it was proved – there are cases of lots of people who are phoney. I mean then it wouldn't work, I can't just do it with all those sorts of people but where I feel in an interview that there is a force there I would use my power of exorcism.

R. Don't you feel that you spend most of your life in danger?

C. I agree that it is dangerous to be an exorcist but I believe at the same time that I am protected. I believe that priests are protected by God in most cases. If ever I used it wrongly than I think it would be more than dangerous.

R. Well, unavoidably we have now arrived at something ecclesiastical. What is your position as regards clerical authority?

C. Well I have for the past five years had a general sanction to perform exorcism . . .

R. From Ramsey???!!!

C. Well, he knows about it. The ex-Archbishop did know that I was doing it and I was placed on this special list at Church House, at the Church Inquiry Office to answer questions on exorcism. But it did come from the Bishop of the diocese here, Bishop Stopford did give me sanction to use exorcism.

R. Although my own upbringing was Roman Catholic I have come to feel much more at home with Anglican priests. Do RCs send people to you?

C. Yes, they do at times.

R. Often?

C. No. But there have been occasions where this has occured. I have had people from the local parish church who've been sent to me.

R. What is their excuse? The Romans are supposed to hold the Keys to the Kingdom.

C. Well, they say that it is very complicated for them to attain an exorcism because they have to go through a lot of channels before it can be done, that in some cases it is urgent and they know that I can do it and they think in these circumstances it might be easier to send the person to me. That's what they have told me.

R, Well, so much for the Keys to the Kingdom. Give me another case history. Well, I'll tell you what: give me mine.

C. Well, when I met you, you were quite clearly under demonic attack. There had been the most extraordinary phenomena in your house up in Yorkshire, as well as in your flat where you were in London. And it was quite clear that there were certain Witches that appeared to be alien to you and were attempting to destroy you. I know it did clear and I think you felt this at the time. That it had cleared sufficiently for you to know in your mind what was happening.

R. Yes. I don't think I was possessed, but I do think I was being attacked.

C. Yes, I think that's right. I wouldn't use the word possessed – I think it was more sort of a 'Witchment' or something.

R. I'm wondering about how much medical assistance you get, qualified I mean.

C. A lot, in some cases. I have had two psychiatrists who have been present when I've done an exorcism. They have brought their own patients. And I've had other doctors present as well, not psychiatrists, ordinary doctors. They are not alien to the idea. Sometimes they welcome the fact that their patient can be helped. And I've had doctors who have sent me patients and they have given evidence afterwards of what has happened and it has usually been very good.

R. What is the percentage of people who need to be exorcised as opposed to the percentage of people who need a good 'shrink'?

C. It is difficult to say because there are some cases where they are mixed up and they need both. There is one psychiatrist who brought me a patient because they had tried various forms of treatment and none had worked. And he said that after this man had been exorcised he could treat him in a way that he couldn't before, because he felt there had been a sort of force gripping that he couldn't get through. But he could get through after the exorcism. However, the man still needed treatment. But I don't think that is the case with a great many people. I think it is simply a spiritual thing in a spiritual dimension.

R. How do you define spiritual things? What is a person's spirit?

C. Well a person's spirit is a departed soul after death. I think a person's spirit is in a different dimension from his mind. And I think this is where an awful lot of mistakes are made. People think that a spiritual condition is a mental condition. For instance, the mind chooses the means towards an end and the spirit chooses *between* ends. And it is a different dimension, and I think people sometimes get caught between identifying one from the other.

R. But spirits don't need bodies.

C. Well, they have to function through a body in the normal way but they are not dependent on them.

R. That's true. What was your scariest exorcism?

C. I think the high priestess Witch exorcism, but I think you've already covered that.*

R. But tell me, why did you become an exorcist?

C. I didn't choose it really. But I did feel that because I had been exorcised that I should be, so to speak, 'saved to serve'.

R. Are you a healer as well?

C. Yes I have done that as well. There are some cases of healing that are scary also.

R. Is healing a form of exorcism?

C. No. I would think it was rather separate. I think with exorcism there is a force there apart from the person whereas with healing you are only dealing with the person.

R. Would you choose to be an exorcist or would you rather live a nice, quiet, simple life?

* See Section IV, page 111.

C. I think I'd rather live a nice, quiet, simple life. I don't really like being an exorcist. In fact I've often thought of giving it all up but I do feel that necessity has laid it upon me. People are so badly in need of this kind of help and it seems almost cruel not to do it.

R. It is probably an important question – Did you ever kill anybody?

C. No. I'm not aware of it.

R. Have you known any cases of anyone being harmed by exorcism?

C. I wouldn't say they have been harmed by it, but they haven't been helped by it. I mean, for instance, there is one case that I was handling with a psychiatrist – a well-known psychiatrist – and the patient committed suicide. I talked it over with the psychiatrist and asked 'Why do you think he committed suicide?' and he said 'Well he probably would have in any case, whether you'd seen him or I'd seen him; it wouldn't have made any difference.' It's quite possible that people might say exorcism might do harm; but so can psychiatry.

R. Can anyone be exorcised against his will?

C. It is *just* conceivably possible that in some cases it would work. I have had one case where a man was exorcised against his will and it later had a rather strange effect.

R. Tell me about it.

C. The man was right outside the Church. This was a very weird thing. One day I was talking at a meeting and somebody got up and asked 'Can a person be exorcised against his will?' and before I was able to answer a man got up from the audience and said 'I was. You did it to me and I was dead alien to it, but a few months later I suddenly changed my whole way of life.'

And at that time he wasn't even in the Church. It was a rather extraordinary thing to occur but I wouldn't say that it was a test case. I would say that it was very rare that someone could be exorcised against his will, but this did in fact happen.

R. Do you do unconscious healing? Sort of pass through the room and suddenly somebody feels better.

C. Well people have said that this has happened but I haven't been conscious of it happening and I've been quite surprised when they've said 'I feel much better' and I can't understand why it should happen.

R. Just one last question – Have you ever lived before?

C. Not that I'm aware of. [*Laughter*] In fact there was an artist who once painted me as what you might call a medieval monk. What exactly she saw I don't know, but I couldn't see it myself.

2   Joan Grant

'And mother said to him [Crowley],
"Crawl, you toad!" And he did!'

— In conversation

'Oh, if only people would realise how dangerous it is not to
love . . .'

— *Many Lifetimes*

Joan Grant is the author of fourteen books, the first among
them the world-famous *Winged Pharaoh*, which has been called
'the greatest novel of reincarnation ever written'. In this
beautiful and lyrical book Miss Grant recounts her own
experiences as a winged pharaoh – a ruler who possesses
psychic powers and has been initiated into the Mysteries – in
Egypt during the First Dynasty. She believes she possesses
what she calls 'the far memory', allowing her to recall her
previous incarnations almost at will. Along with her
psychiatrist husband she treats two patients a day in her flat
in Kensington, many of whom suffer from karmic disturbance
resulting from a mistake or traumatic experience which
occured in a previous incarnation. In her treatments Miss
Grant never assumes immediately that this is the case;
however she does feel that many persons suffering from
apparently physical ailments are actually recalling a similar
affliction suffered in a previous lifetime. Including,
apparently, myself.

Miss Grant is very beautiful and singularly tough-minded.
Genuine occultists are usually the most practical people in the
world. Her grey hair done up in a bun, her eyes like pebbles
under clear water alert to everything around and inside her,

she is both charming and disarmingly candid. Her IQ is not for public knowledge, but she relaxes by playing 3-dimensional chess – which she and one of her husbands invented – and winning. She will not tolerate phoney occultists (in fact I've never heard her use the word 'occultist') and gives them short shrift. But she herself is amazingly psychic, a healer, and moves between her Egyptian incarnations and her present one with all the ease of a young girl riding a bicycle. She wears green a lot. It suits her.

There is in and about every human face and, for that matter, the faces of animals a quality which tells one a great deal about the person inside. Appearances really are not deceptive, if one only learns how to look. Great painters know this well. A self-portrait by Rembrandt can be very painful if you look at it steadily. Leonardo could capture eternal ecstacy in the human face of an angel, and Botticelli a paradoxically earthy transcendence; in his *Primavera,* the portraits are all very sensual, but although their feet are touching the ground all the characters seem to be floating. Psychics can discern the aura, which is a field of force surrounding the human body, sometimes of one predominant colour, often of many.

Chain-smoking from a cigarette box that was obviously made for her (a book-sized wooden box whose lid is carved as a replica of the cover of the original edition of *Winged Pharaoh*); observing you with a smile and a sidelong glance to see if you've grasped the humour of what she has just said; or busily serving up an elegant cold supper with a *sauce vinaigrette* which, since you requested it, she has miraculously concocted in just under three minutes; or seeing a patient: Joan Grant's face is truly radiant. 'Nobody,' her husband told me, 'ever speaks with her and leaves without being better off in some way.'

JG. What do you mean, you're a Witch?
RD. Well, I was initiated by a genuine Witch who had the status which allowed her to initiate.
JG. [*Silence*]
RD. [*Coughs*]
JG. [*Longer silence*]
RD. Ah yes; well, speaking of psychic attack, I believe your

sister was once attacked by Aleister Crowley.

JG. Bit of sorcery. [*This word is pronounced with scorn.*] He was a man with filthy habits. *Filthy* habits. We met him before a cruise on the *Lusitania*. In New York. And he had his eye on my sister. One day she and I were sitting in a room and he walked up to us. He took out his tie pin and proceeded to jab it in her wrist. Then he wiped the blood on to his handkerchief and told her, 'Aha, my proud beauty! Now I have you in my power.'

RD. He *said* this???!!!

JG. Those were his words, more or less.

RD. No wonder his prose is so purple. What happened then?

JG. Fortunately mother, who was very powerful, walked in to the room at that moment and saw what happened. Of course, she was furious. She stormed up to us. And mother said to him, 'Crawl, you toad!' And he did! On all fours, out of the room. Then mother said, 'Well, I guess I know how to take care of my cubs.'

RD. Have you ever performed an exorcism? We'll get on to your definition of exorcism later.

JG. Well, I've laid spooks, if you'll pardon the expression. Shall I tell you about a spook in a church we got rid of once?

RD. Spooks give me the creeps, but I guess we're on to the subject of exorcising places. Please go on.

JG. They give me the creeps, too. I went into this church in South Wales; it was interdenominational at the time but had been consecrated before the Reformation – it was very old. And I spotted this spook priest over in the corner, to the left of the altar, face down on the floor and struggling for some reason. He appeared to be trapped in the place. He was probably a bishop because he was holding a crosier. So I asked my friend G— if he would say a mass in the church for the soul of this spook. We arranged it with the local vicar, and G— began to say the mass. A mass, you know, properly understood, is not just an isolated priest and two assistants mumbling some prayers while the people look on. *Attendants* at mass have to be just that, they have to participate. I had once asked G—, 'How many times have you attended a mass that was truly effective?' He 'said, 'One time in about four

58

hundred.' I said, 'Have you ever performed one?' He said, 'No.' But this time something remarkable happened. The local vicar was attending the mass and during the ceremony he was seized by some force or other and toppled, at the communion rail, on to the floor. He assumed the position in which I had first seen the spook, and out of nowhere a crosier appeared in his hand.

RD. Did everyone see this?

JG. 3 out of 4, or so.

RD. Was there an actual crosier in the church at the time?

JG. No, hadn't been for years. That's what made it so interesting. We went on with the mass, the vicar came to himself again, and the spirit seems to have been freed. Along with the crosier.

RD. Have you ever performed anything similar on a living human being?

JG. Well, a young patient was staying with us once and I gradually figured out that his anxieties were rooted in a previous incarnation. He had been a cleric too, you see, and what he needed was to receive the sacraments. So I fixed him a glass of port and got a biscuit and charged them both.

RD. Charged them?

JG. I put my hands over the stuff and charged it with my will. It was a sort of Eucharist, really, though I didn't tell him anything about it because he wouldn't have understood. Then I took the charged wine and wafer up to his room. He was in bed at the time, and I said, 'You're looking rather coldish, you'd better have some port. Oh, and you'd better have a biscuit too, these are very good.' He had the wine and biscuit and went to sleep. He began to come round after that. I wrote about it in *Many Lifetimes*.

RD. You're obviously a natural psychic, as opposed to someone who has to train to develop his psychic faculties. Presumably, you've been psychic since birth.

JG. Yes, but I soon learned to shut up about it. I remember once, as a small girl, there were about two hundred guests in the house and I came down from my room in my nightdress to say goodnight. As I was going back up the stairs I saw a cat.

RD. I like black cats.

JG. Yes, I can imagine you would. But this one wasn't black.* Well as I began stroking the cat one of the guests, a woman, came up and asked me what I was doing and I began to describe the cat to her. 'Is it your cat?' I asked her. 'Yes,' she said, 'and it died last week.' Upset the poor woman terribly.

RD. As well as being a pyshic, you, in collaboration with your husband who holds several degrees, do a great deal of what is regarded as 'legitimate' therapy. Would you care to comment on the aspects of possession, or obsession if you like, and your methods of treatment? Some would call the process of relieving a patient 'exorcism'. Could you comment on that as well?

JG. Well, you can find my definition of spooks in our book, *Many Lifetimes,* also a lot of accounts of my husband's and my treatments.† Exorcism is not really my scene, you know. But often by discovering the trouble in a past life one can do a great deal of good by releasing anxieties in a living person which are otherwise totally inexplicable. I mention an incident which occured in Brussels when I was about twenty. My husband and his friends had gone out of our hotel for the evening but as I was too tired to join them, I had a hot bath and went to bed. Suddenly a young man darted out of the bathroom and before I had time to do anything he flung himself out of the window. I was horrified, of course, but when I forced myself to look out of the window there was no corpse, just a man carrying a load of bottles – a waiter. And the incident kept repeating itself, until I managed to unite with this man and absorb his fear and release him. The point of all this for your purposes I suppose is that, as I also mention in the book, had someone inhabited that room for several years he might have found he had developed an unexplainable fear of heights. He would have needed treatment.

* Author's presumption. A tortoise shell with four white paws. Power of suggestion?
† *Many Lifetimes,* Denys Kelsey and Joan Grant (see Bibliography). 'A ghost is a dissociated fragment of a personality which has become split off from the rest, and it remains self-imprisoned in a timeless present, whilst the integrated components continue the normal process of evolution . . . So long as a ghost remains extant, it can impinge upon a subsequent personality and may be responsible for irrational fears, compulsive behaviour, or psychosomatic conditions.'

RD. Had such a suicide taken place in that room?

JG. Just several days earlier.

RD. I'd call that an exorcism. An exorcism of a place, as well as a person. And the treatment of this hypothetical person who lived in the room for several years, I'd call that an exorcism as well.

JG. Hmmm. I think there's something wrong with your legs. Is there?

RD. Yes.

JG. Well there seems to be a great deal of pain. I see you dying in 1942 or thereabouts, and something crumbling away in a bomb blast or something and falling on your legs – here . . . and here.* And you have trouble with your thighs.

RD. Yes.

JG. You struggled to get out of the wreckage in order to escape something – water, or maybe fire – and died a rather horrific death.

RD. I was reborn in '44 . . .

JG. Well, sometimes people come back rather quickly by choice to get on with it – passing the bucket, and all that.

RD. If someone were, say, to attack me psychically, might they choose my legs as the easiest target? The weakest point of defence?

JG. Feasible, yes.

RD. Originally I was going to call this book *Sane Exorcism* but didn't because of Dion Fortune's book, *Sane Occultism* . . .

JG. Oh, *her!* . . .

[*Enforced silence. Kenneth Tynan once wrote of Hemingway that he sometimes had the knack of 'not only closing the subject but sitting on the lid'.*]

RD. But *Sane Occultism* is a good book. So is *Psychic Self-Defense*. . . . Well, I won't press you right now on that. Sometime, certainly, but not now. Anyway, the reason I mentioned this is that in *Many Lifetimes* you give a lovely definition of sanity which I think applies to the book in general. Your book certainly, and mine I hope. Would you care to quote it?

JG. 'Sanity is the ability to see things as they really are.'

* Absolutely correct as to the place of pain.

3   Robert Mortimer, Bishop of Exeter, Retired

'[Exorcism is] an extension of the frontiers of Christ's kingdom . . .'

The Reverend Robert Mortimer retired two years ago as Bishop of Exeter and now ministers in Penrith in the Lake District. But while serving as Bishop in 1963, he convened a commission of Anglican and Roman Catholic priests to discuss the subject of exorcism and its place in the church and society as a whole. The commission, of which Michael Ramsey, not yet Archbishop of Canterbury, thoroughly disapproved, produced a remarkable report which unfortunately had to be trimmed to publishable size and appeared as the pamphlet *Exorcism,* still the most useful reference work on Christian exorcism available. The report was edited by Dom Robert Petitpierre, OSB, an experienced exorcist.

RD. Reverend Mortimer, how did you become interested in so controversial – as it was in 1963 – a subject as exorcism?
RM. Well, of course the press reportage was disturbing, even then. And as bishop I was receiving letters, even phonecalls, asking advice on how to handle cases where exorcism appeared to be necessary. And I was appalled to learn that so many of my clergymen knew little or nothing at all about the subject.
RD. You speak of *positive* exorcism . . .
RM. Yes. As I say in the pamphlet, the positive aspect of exorcism involves a demonstration of the Church's power to beat down evil influences and, above all, replace them with good, I used the phrase 'extension of the frontiers of Christ's

kingdom'.

RD. Baptism, for example.

RM. Yes, quite.

RD. 'Positive exorcism' is a rather unique idea.

RM. Well perhaps it is, but although exorcism is not usually regarded as a sacrament it does play a part in sacramental operations; baptism, for example, as you mentioned.

RD. A fair number of theologians have decided that exorcism is outmoded and should be removed from Christian practice. Do you think this will happen?

RM. No. But the practice will come under some form of regulation. So it's all to the good in the long run.

RD. What about the Taylor case?

RM. Well obviously, they didn't know what they were doing. Which only supports my point. You mentioned an apparent contradiction in the pamphlet.* Well what we were saying there, that it is possible for a lay person or even a non-Christian to exorcise, and yet at the same time exorcism is an operation of the Church, although it was inaccurately phrased, means that more needs to be known by everyone about the subject but that some form of organizational control is necessary. If one is to avoid such tragedies as that of the Taylors.

RD. And yet the non-Christian is described as being able to exorcise only 'in the name of Christ'. Do you believe in non-Christian exorcism?

RM. Well, I know very little about it.

RD. Did you know there is such a thing as Satanist exorcism?

RM. Good Lord, no. I recognize a distinction between Black and White magic, but I've never heard of anything of that sort and know very little about Witchcraft. As I've pointed out, the need for exorcism is usually more apparent in countries that are recently converted from paganism than in countries with a strong Christian tradition.

Just across the road from the hotel in which I was staying during my visit to the Reverend Mortimer and, for the first time, the Lake District, there is a site known to the locals as

* See earlier, Part II, chapter 1, p. 21.

'King Arthur's Table'. It consists of two circular mounds surrounded by a trench, with two levelled-off entrances to the outer circle. Dating back to 1800 BC, it is clearly a place of heathen worship. ('Heathen' refers merely to 'those who worship on the heath'; similarly 'pagan' stems from the Latin *paganus,* one who lives in the country, that is, one of those ancient peasants whom Christian missionaries, who preached mostly in the cities, had not reached yet.) It is a perfect Witches' circle, very like the ones drawn by modern Witches. Behind the hotel in a wooded area are the remains of a Druidic mound, whose stones have mostly been pirated away but whose shape is unmistakably circular. If the Reverend Mortimer is correct and modern Witchcraft is flourishing more than ever before, from his viewpoint at least the need for exorcism must indeed exist in Britain, a country which resisted Christian conversion for some time.

Robert Mortimer, a tall, thin, grey-haired man who, in purple vest, Roman collar and austere grey suit, cannot better be described than as one who looks like he *ought* to be a bishop, has a marvellous sense of humour. When I and my companion arrived the day before the interview – I dressed like a flash American author in green velvet suit, beige jumper and shades, with ankh prominent on my chest; she looking like every man's dream of Lady Brett Ashley – and with very little luggage, the small family hotel outside Penrith looked a little appalled. When I ordered breakfast in the room and a bottle of cold white wine to go with it, it was obvious to the staff that the days of Sodom and Gomorrah were not yet over. I wasn't even trying to be funny the next morning when I approached reception and said, 'Oh, by the way, the retired Bishop of Exeter will be joining us at midday today,' but the look on the receptionist's face was worth a thousand Academy Awards. He probably figured that for the two of us a normal parish priest wasn't enough and we needed at least a bishop to straighten us out or maybe the Archbishop of Canterbury working in league with the Pope. When the Reverend Mortimer actually showed up, wearing a massive bishop's ring of amethyst set in gold on his index finger and looking as I have described him, one would have thought the joint was to

64

be exorcised at a stroke. All that was lacking were the robes, mitre and crosier. A truly humble man, he found the whole scene quite amusing, as staff and clientele alike reacted to his quiet but imposing presence. And the unlikely company he was keeping.

The rest of the interview took place at the Sharrow Bay Country House Hotel, to which the Reverend Mortimer drove us. The dining room overlooks Lake Ullswater, and as we lunched on Vichysoisse, salmon mousse, pork with a superb Cumberland sauce, excellently prepared fresh vegetables, salad, coffee ices, fruit, coffee and brandy, I was beginning to feel a little unworldly. African violets graced the table and anemones came with dessert. The Reverend Mortimer and my companion had an excellent view of the lake, where an unlucky water skier was annoying the Reverend with the noise of his towing boat. The skier kept falling over.

'Oh, perhaps he'll drown,' said the Reverend after a particularly disastrous-looking spill. The man re-surfaced. 'Drat,' said the Reverend to my companion, 'he didn't.'

RD. Do you come here often?
RM. Oh, heavens no. Never been near the place. Just heard about it. Five star. Shouldn't think I could afford it.
RD. Well, I guess advance royalties on the book should almost cover this.
COMPANION. Quite.

RD. Did you encounter any resistance within the church itself to your convening a commission on exorcism?
RM. Well, Michael [Ramsey] didn't approve, and I don't suppose he's changed his mind much. It was a lot of fun. Dom Robert, for example, who tends to differ with people quite a bit – he once had a rather boisterous quarrel with his own abbot – is a remarkably stimulating man to be around. About six of us at a time would get together and discuss exorcism, and we determined our views on the theology underlying the rite and in the end we drew up a programme for the training of clergy in the field.
RD. How did you get the pamphlet published?

65

RM. You might well ask. In the end we had quite a large report and Dom Robert honed it down. There was some opposition.

RD. Would you say that the real danger of exorcism lies in the ritual itself, as prescribed by the church, or in the incompetence of the exorcist?

RM. More in the latter.

RD. You have said that you yourself are not an exorcist, and yet your commission did more work to illuminate the subject than any orthodox church group has done since the eighteenth century. Do you feel that exorcism is mostly power of suggestion?

RM. Quite often it is, yes. Many people who believe they're possessed are not. We assembled a number of blessings whereby a priest can comfort a disturbed person . . .

RD. So possession can be purely subjective, if that's not a contradiction in terms?

RM. Well, it is you know, but disturbances of this sort often are purely subjective. Yet the rite of exorcism often seems to quiet the person's mind.

RD. In your opinion – to bring up the Taylor case again – should a person be examined medically and psychiatrically before he is exorcised?

RM. Yes.

RD. Do demons really exist, though, outside the human mind?

RM. [*Pause*] Yes. Yes, they do.

The retired Bishop of Exeter drove us back to our own hotel before departing the following morning for Devon, his old bishopric. ('I'm going down to bless a new organ, or something – at least, that's the excuse I'm using.') Clearly, he misses the excitement of such activities as convening a commission of experts on exorcism. I asked his blessing for myself and my friend and he gave it.

4 Françoise Strachan

'This system of healing, which has been Divinely revealed unto us, shows that it is our fears, our cares, our anxieties and such like that open the path to the invasion of illness . . .'

'And . . . the disease, no matter what it is, will leave us.'
– Dr Edward Bach

When Françoise Strachan met with me to do this interview I was bending over a huge ceremonial sword which lay on a bench in Swiss Cottage tube station. I had brought the sword with me to give to Miss Strachan, so that she in turn could give it to her friend George Alexander, who makes magical equipment. The sword, of Excalibur proportions, had been hand-forged by my friend Chris Gosselin, and I needed the handle changed to match that of my athame. George was obviously the man to do it. But in my haste to make the appointment with Françoise I had neglected to wrap the sword and was beginning to notice the strange looks people were giving me and the wide girth I was being allotted in an otherwise crowded tube station. With a hastily purchased *Guardian* I was trying to conceal the nature of the 'dangerous' weapon I was carrying. Ritual knives and swords, by the way, with the exception of a white-handled knife used for special purposes may never be used except ritualistically and certainly not for clobbering anybody, so everyone was safe. Then I gradually became aware, as I fumbled away trying to wrap a newspaper around an instrument the size of a large rifle, of someone standing over me, regarding me with the amused detachment with which one watches somebody who is obviously potty. She had large dark eyes, black, straight hair

67

and a kind, inquisitive face. 'I am not,' she said finally, 'carrying *that* thing around with me.'

In retrospect, I'm rather surprised. Miss Strachan has a delightfully impish sense of humour and, as the sword almost matches her in height, I'm sure that the sight of her walking into the office of some publisher who owed her money, carrying a deadly-looking weapon the size of herself, would have brought about a most satisfactory reaction; if not in monetary satisfaction, at least in the look on the face of the receptionist. Françoise is a refreshing phenomenon at a time when the subject of the supernatural has become a public fetish. She is a genuine, but renegade occultist. She refuses labels, though I shall risk incurring her wrath by calling her a healer and expert on exorcism. She moves around occult circles like a bee, rarely stinging but always leaving everyone a little uneasy because of her healthy scepticism. Paradoxically, in a field which has always been overrun with egomaniacs, her open-faced cheekiness and obvious goodwill are her greatest defences. Warmth, not heat, is the first sensation one experiences in her presence.

Casting Out the Devils, her book on exorcism, is a classic in the field. No one interested in exorcism can possibly be without it. It is not a recent book, but is still extremely comprehensive. Although I have tried in this work to be predominantly practical and contemporary rather than historically minded, I have found it impossible in places not to echo Françoise Strachan. One cannot discuss Judaeo-Christianity without occasionally quoting the Bible!

After it was decided that *I* should carry the sword, its point still protruding rather menacingly from the folds of the *Guardian,* we proceeded to a friend's flat where for four hours we talked. I regret, for the reader's sake, that space will not permit me to transcribe the whole conversation. But Miss Strachan's utterly iconoclastic views, supported by her healing record, should be quite evident from the interview here. Her methods get excellent results. She's a healer and exorcist; and what she has to say has been proven, by medically documented evidence, to be true.

RD. How do you know when someone is genuinely 'possessed'?

FS. Initially you might suspect something about the aura, that there's an entity there, but the person doesn't really want to investigate to find out, because somehow the entity lulls them into a state of quiescence. I have offered sometimes to help someone and they say, Oh, no, I'm all right. Like the person we're talking about right now*... and she got quite violent.

RD. Have you ever performed an exorcism? Other interviewers have tried to trap you into this question.

FS. Well, I haven't used bell book and candle, and I haven't used a ritualistic form such as casting circles and such things, but through the work I do with Radionics and the equipment that I use I can gradually eliminate the negative forces in the physical body and the auric structure which surrounds every human body by beaming positive forces, gradually breaking up the negative energies; in other words, I do it by tuning in to the body and dislodging the negative forces or spirit energies or thought forms or whatever happens to be in the aura, through radiation. Rather than invocation.

RD. You say 'gradually'. This must take a lot of patience. A total reluctance to give up.

FS. Well a lot of people do take time. It takes a long time to really clean somebody up totally.

RD. But about 'invocation'...

FS. Sometimes there isn't time to do things gradually. On those particular occasions you have to do some form of inward meditation or something totally separate as well. Also, sometimes it can be helpful if the person wears some form of protective talisman or amulet.

RD. So much for theory. Describe a case history.

FS. There was a case of a young man, who kept on wanting to commit suicide. He was about nineteen. He had been to psychiatrists and none of them could find any particular thing that was bugging him. One of his parents contacted me and asked if I could do anything about this boy. So I checked on the equipment that I have, the sensitive equipment, and I found that every main centre of his brain was blocked with

* See Section IV.

either thought forms, spirits, or something – and I also checked up on his auric body and his glandular system and found that he had a complete attachment – a total invasion of negative forces in different parts of his body.

RD. You say 'invasion'. Do you mean to imply that he was actually invaded by exterior spirit forces? Or did he create these thought forms himself?

FS. Both. Some were thought forms that he'd actually created himself since early childhood; some were things that happened that might have caused a traumatic shock when he was young; and some adverse influences from outside as well. Some were self-created, some were external.

RD. And they got on beautifully together.

FS. Yes. Anyway, I worked on the centres of the brain first of all, because if the brain is affected, this is the most important thing, and the rest of the body can wait a little while. So I worked on the brain and within a very short period of time I also used some flower remedies. You see, when a person has some form of possession they have a form of mental weakness as well, which, let's say, allows the thing to *get in*. And I also worked on the seven chakras in the brain, cleansed them, because I've now discovered there are seven chakras in the brain, as well as seven psychic senses or chakras in the body. So I worked on the seven major centres in the brain, and when they were cleared out, there was no more of the suicide business. He was a bit moody for a while – you can't expect miracles – but gradually he has begun to enjoy life, to go out, to do things he hasn't done before. So it would seem that those forces were pressing on certain thought patterns in the brain, trying to influence him to do away with himself.

RD. As opposed to the traditional 'Begone, Satan' routine, your method seems quite – well, methodical. Ever know anybody who used the old methods?

FS. I've known people who said they did. Quite a few – you know, during the course of researching *Casting Out the Devils*. And I have no doubt that it's true. But I don't buy it.

RD. When we talk about situations in which exorcism is useful: would you regard the patient's condition as, at least, psychosomatic?

70

FS. I think that a lot of thought forms, a lot of entities and influences – I differentiate between them because a lot of these disturbing creatures are self created thought forms, some are thought forms projected by somebody else, and some are totally independent influences, 'real' entities which might have come from a pre-natal experience, for example –

RD. Want to expand on that?

FS. Through the womb, through birth. One can be possessed before birth.

RD. Welcome to *Rosemary's Baby?*

FS. Very funny. But it is seriously true that if the mother has sex with someone who is undesirable a spirit might have been transmitted through somebody and remained in the womb and affected the unborn child. I've done a lot of work on this: psychic pre-natal care. It is possible to tune into a woman's body before her child is born to find out whethet the child's aura is clean.

RD. Hmmm. I asked you earlier how you knew if someone was possessed. Am I possessed?

FS. You've got some negative forces bothering you, yes. But as you asked me, what do you mean by 'possessed'? The Russians have now proved positively that the aura does exist. It is a very delicate organism and it can be disturbed in many ways. Atomic fallout, number one. Traumatic emotional experiences, drugs, pre-natal experience. It's not pretty to say, but it's true: no one I've checked is totally without disturbance, without problems in their chakras.

RD. Françoise, what in hell is a chakra?

FS. Chakras are the psychic centres. In Japan there is a doctor who now works on the chakras, which are like the taps between the outer world and the inner world. If these centres of energy are depleted, all the organs in the physical body become depleted as well. Anything can cause a disturbance of the chakras, even a simple physical accident. So you don't have to play with a ouija board or attend a seance or summon a demon to experience psychic disturbance. You don't have to go anywhere near the occult.

RD. This may strike some readers as rather disturbing. Then what is the 'devil'?

FS. To me, evil or 'devil' is a build-up of anti-life force or negative energy. Jung talks about the shadow side or the dark side of an individual, and he refers to it as the unregenerated side of the psyche. But these forces of which I'm speaking are anti-life forces in the universe, self-created or external, which latch on to static energy in an individual. If a person's aura is weak, they can invade it. Like attracts like. If we create an artificial ego instead of realizing that the life force, God, good, or whatever you want to call it, is flowing through us, we isolate ourselves. But if we flow *with* this universal harmony we don't create these problems. And probably it's because we isolate ourselves and think that our personal importance is more significant than these total life forces that we fail to, as the red Indians say, walk in balance. All these rubber shoes, this concrete . . . I honestly believe that one of the main causes of possession is man's lack of contact with nature.

RD. Which creates disharmony?

FS. Yes. This may be a funny thing to say, but all this rubber-soled shoe business – leather is so expensive these days – and all the building materials that surround us every minute, they all have their effect and weaken the aura.

RD. Where else could they have staged *The Exorcist* but in Washington? And *Rosemary's Baby* but New York?

FS. Well, then of course you can't just go off in the woods and say forget everything.

RD. Considering which, what practical suggestions would you like to give about avoiding possession?

FS. Well, let's put it this way. The mind should be like a reflecting point or a reflecting mirror for the Self-consciousness to reflect through the body. You can call the Self-consciousness pure Light, pure Love, pure Energy – it doesn't matter what you call it – pure Consciousness that should flow through the mind. Now if this is not happening, and there are obstructions there, as through hate, fear, jealousy, lust, cruelty, then these are obstructions in the mind, and they'll stop the pure force of Love, of the soul energies flowing through you, and create a breeding ground for possessing forces or demons or whatever you'd like to call them. I have never yet had the pleasure of meeting anyone

72

entirely free of these weaknesses.

RD. So anyone's prey to possession?

FS. Don't be paranoid. What I'm working with now are the discoveries of Dr Edward Bach.* Through his sensitivity and sympathy with nature, he has discovered several cures by which the flower remedies I mentioned earlier gradually heal the mind, and the mind heals the body of every tension imaginable. No use of drugs, or any artificial stimulae. So the pure consciousness can flow through from the soul, and healing occurs. Because the mind isn't distorted. I'm treating causes, not effects; or trying to. To prevent what you call possession.

RD. Then what in your opinion should an exorcist be? A doctor or a priest?

FS. Really an exorcist should be both doctor and priest. There are doctors of souls as well as bodies.

RD. How many of those do you know?

FS. I'm afraid, not over a dozen.

Françoise Strachan is a member of the centre for Psychic Health Research, B/M Spiritos, London WC1V 6XX. Anyone wishing to contact her for further information may do so c/o this address.

* Edward Bach, MB, BS, MRCS, LRCP, DPH. See *The Twelve Healers*, C. W. Daniel, London, 1974.

PART IV
Sane exorcism

All the documented case histories which follow were, I have reason to believe, instances of genuine possession. The first concerns a psychic attack; the next two describe the not-infrequent occasions when discarnate human spirits take possession of living human beings for their own ends; the last, an exorcism performed by the Reverend Neil-Smith on a (Black) Witch High Priestess, may be called, according to your beliefs and experience of the subject, either an instance of manic hysteria or a manifestation of true demonism.

1   The case of the attacked author

Totally ignorant of the occult, I was once in love and having an affair with a beautiful young woman who said she believed she was a Witch. I learned later – much later – that she was in fact a Witch and a very powerful one, an adept, initiated in the Celtic tradition. We were living together very happily, I at the time feeling that Witchcraft belonged somewhere back in the twelfth century but perfectly willing to put up with all this kookiness because of the girl's beauty, kindness, our love for one another, and her obvious sincerity in her beliefs. I might add that any healthy male reader who ever laid eyes on her would understand that if she suddenly walked into the room over breakfast and decided to call herself a jet-propelled broomstick he would say, 'Oh yes,' and get on with his bacon and eggs. This affair was in fact the prelude to my first experience of psychic attack. About that I was more sceptical – as a major at University in Rationalist philosophy, lapsed Catholic, devout materialist and agnostic (if that's possible), thoroughly confused and disappointed with religion in general – than anyone holding this book could be.

Not until she began to try to kill herself and me and to go into trances from which I could not awaken her; not until her features and voice began to alter to a remarkable extent and, pentagrams appeared on the floors and ceilings of rooms which no one had entered; not until dogs started baying in the middle of the night outside second-storey windows and strange Negros (she had never known a Negro) appeared at her office insisting they were friends of hers and refusing to leave until they had seen her – to confront her, as I am now aware, with the Evil Eye or perhaps a talisman of destruction; not until a car identical to hers parked in the office lot blew up, nearly injuring the unsuspecting secretary who was its owner; it was not until all this had occurred that I had to admit to the possibility that something, maybe just something, was a little weird about the whole situation.

Paul Huson, a Witch High Priest and author of two excellent occult books listed in the Bibliography, has given one of the sanest and at the same time most accurate descriptions of the symptoms of this form of psychic attack. As I could not describe them better, I shall merely quote him:

> Apart from unpleasant vibrations and general miasmas of hostility or fear, the symptoms of a magical attack can range from severe, recurrent nightmares, through runs of unbelievably bad luck, psychosomatic disturbances and allergies, often accompanied by poltergeist manifestations, to outright cases of lunacy or sudden death.

Huson is a highly skilled and experienced occultist, as well as a walking library on the subject of occultism; in other words, a rational and therefore sceptical man. So he immediately appends:

> Of course, all of these things, bar the poltergeist phenomena, can and in the case of the nonwitch generally do have a definitely nonoccult basis. As such, it is always best to consult a regular doctor or psychiatrist before assuming any form of psychic attack.

This is, and must always be, the guideline to assessing whether a genuine psychic attack is taking place or whether a mild prescription of Valium might not do the trick. There are times, rarely, but there are times when the *only* way of seeing what is happening is as a psychic attack.

Take this case, for example. Pentagrams appear chalked with menacing Hebrew inscriptions in places where no one has been and, in any case, there is no chalk in the house. The woman with whom you are living and think you know very well, who has had a life-long fear of putting her head under water, is found naked in the bathtub trying to drown herself. She develops the rather annoying habit of throwing objects at your head and muttering, or yelling, obscenities when previously she could not tolerate any form of smut. And, on one particularly memorable occasion, she strolls, dressed only in her nightgown, in a trance state out into the middle of the M4. No doctor would be troubled with such a nutty story at 2 am; on the other hand no half-asleep lorry driver, seeing a lady in a nightgown two feet in front of his truck, would have much time to consider the situation either. On such occasions hesitation would be tantamount to murder. Instant action is not only necessary but delay would be morally indefensible.

On a recent television show, a smug Roman Catholic priest voiced the opinion that no sane, healthy, religious member of his church who took the sacraments regularly could possibly suffer so dire a fate as possession. I wish to heaven, to hell, to my Gods and his that he were correct. But too many factual cases prove him wrong. The particular case I am describing here, however, involved someone delving deeply into occult pursuits; so I shall give a description of the symptoms peculiar to such a situation and end with a ritual, never before published, which may be of use in these circumstances.

Needless to say, as one inexperienced and previously uninterested in occultism, the sudden change which overwhelmed – and nearly killed – my friend terrified me thoroughly. Nevertheless, because I loved and still do love her, I was certainly not going to leave her alone in that condition unless absolutely necessary. But affairs in Yorkshire forced me to be away for some days. So she taught me the formula of a pentagram of protection, which is easy to find in the *Lemegeton* or *Lesser Key of Solomon,* and need not be repeated here. I worked with this pentagram sketched on the wood floor of my bedroom sometimes for nights on end.

One morning I received a telegram. DEUTCH. YOU ARE TOO LATE. SHE SEEMS A WILLING VICTIM. It was signed by a name known to many occultists. My friend had informed me as well, on my departure, of a method of nullifying such menacing communications, and I employed it.

By now I was living from night to day, hoping for cheques to arrive from editors so that I need not distract myself writing articles, my energy draining slowly. This was ominous enough, as was the fact that, although I am a pretty good beer drinker, a half pint of Yorkshire bitter would leave me utterly exhausted and in the end I had to stop drinking entirely and resort to ice lollies to restore my energy. By then I realized that, like it or not, I was involved with the occult.

I believed, and still believe, that one should either know nothing whatever of these matters or as much as one can possibly learn; I already knew *something*. Whether you believe in or are 'into' the occult, when under psychic attack you are definitely *in* it. To paraphrase Paul Huson again and describe, as succinctly as possible, the symptoms of psychic attack, 'Man, it's like you're on a bad acid trip. Only, you ain't had no acid.'

I continued receiving threatening telegrams and unsigned letters daily, which, believe it or not, after a period of a week or so became about as frightening as milk bills or demands for payment on a subscription to *Reader's Digest* which you cancelled years ago. I simply woke up on the floor in front of the pentagram, walked downstairs to gulp a mouthful of milk and went to the front door to see what kind of a curse had arrived in the mail. To this day, except that they came from London, I do not know from where or whom these heartening little gems were sent.

With the permission of the writer, the girl in this case, I am reproducing one of the letters I received from her during this period. She has no record of emotional disturbance, no psychiatric history; she had a normal childhood and is in no way disturbed at the present time. The S referred to in the letter is Stewart Farrar, Witch High Priest and author of an excellent book on Witchcraft, *What Witches Do*. The girl in question had done some Witch workings with his coven.

My friend's distraught state is clearly indicated not only by the content and handwriting on the letter, but by the fact that this short message took nearly two hours to write.

She must have been able to pull herself together for a little while at some stage, however. Two mornings later, along with a hair-raising curse in the handwriting of whomever had been

Hi

22/9/72.
7.00pm

This is just to let you know
that ████████ was here this evening.
He's just left. Ludicrous as it
may seem I've a feeling that
you might not know about it
otherwise. It may seem silly to you
but I've a feeling about tomorrow. Still
as so many things seem to have
happened perhaps you will understand.
██████ left the ritual with me
but wouldn't stay in the
room because he said there were
conflicting forces.

The ritual involves water, salt,
athame and a naked me. He left
me an athame which he says I
mustn't show to anybody — that's a
bit unusual. Under normal circumstances the High Priest would perform it
for the female or the High Priestess for
the male. The cleaning is called
Opening of the Body and is supposed to
be able to ward off ~~the~~ all
~~a~~ PSYChic aTTaCK.

79

Somehow, even as I write, I
feel unable to perform the
ritual.
Perhaps I have some sort
of self-destructive instinct.
This seems to HAVE
TAKEN ME A LONG TIME TO
WRITE — IT'S NOW 8.50 AM.
I THINK I'LL GO AND
POST THIS

Blessed
BE!

filling my mail with invective quoted — Biblical scholars take
note — from Psalms, I received the invocation on page 81, a
blessing from the girl.

The behaviour of Stewart Farrar and his coven on this
occasion was, to put it mildly, a little unusual. Upon
initiation, Witches take a vow always to help other members
of the Craft. Although the girl was not officially a member of
Farrar's coven, she had worked with the group often,
occasionally serving as a medium — not a happy task or one
undertaken lightly — for their workings. Except for presenting
an obviously hysterical lady with a black-handled knife and
then fleeing the scene, neither Farrar nor his High Priestess
lifted a finger to help her.

Later, after the attack had begun on me in earnest and I

In Perfect Love and Perfect Trust
     Blessed Be

I conjure and pray ye, O ye
Angels of God and ye Celestial
Spirits to come into mine aid;
come and behold the Signs
of Thane, and be my witness
before the sovereign lords of the
watchtowers of the disobedience
of these evil and fallen
spirits who were at one
time my companions.

Protect His Name

had rejoined the girl in London, we met with Farrar's group to discuss the situation. One of the female Witches, who had laid eyes on me no more than five minutes earlier, accused me of being a con man who was using the girl. (To what end I cannot imagine; we neither of us had any money.) Another accused me of being a vampire. They all refused categorically to help the girl. Admittedly, since I was not a Witch, they were under no obligation to help me; but, seeing that I was obviously in a state of nervous exhaustion, there was no particular reason to insult me unjustly either. Personally I believe that if someone arrives at my door and says, 'I'm possessed: will you help me?', I should interpret this as 'I'm scared out of my wits: will you help me?', invite him in for a cup of tea and then try to determine what the real problem is. As a Witch or as a human being I would feel obliged to do this. Refusing help outright to a friend, a fellow-Witch, or even a total stranger, is not or should not be what Witches do.

Faced with a problem of this nature and equipped with no knowledge of the Unseen is like being handed a time bomb in the middle of Piccadilly Circus marked '*Going off in 2 seconds*'. Before I could return to London to meet, however fruitlessly, with the Farrar coven, I continued to work on the pentagram, my physical and mental stamina weakening daily. Should anyone reading this book experience any of the symptoms I experienced and am about to describe, he should immediately consult a physician, a psychiatrist, or a clergyman he trusts who has some knowledge of exorcism. Paranoia under totally unfamiliar circumstances is the main and sometimes the most difficult thing to avoid. The attacker intends to create fear and, for as long as possible, to disguise its real source.

> The first really telltale signs are the periodical nightmares and general sense of evil in the air. The dreams will generally have a specific motif repeated ad nauseam with minor variations on the theme.*

The worst occurrences of the first stages of psychic attack usually come at night. Later on, if the attack is sufficiently

* Paul Huson, *Mastering Witchcraft*.

powerful or not neutralized with enough force, they may come at any time. From my experience, the time to look out for is from just after sundown until 3 am, when the attacks seem to lose momentum.

I continued to work on the pentagram; since the threats continued to appear in the mail ('Give us this day our daily curse'?) I assumed that my working must be having some effect, at least to the extent of annoying the attackers so that they felt it necessary to continue trying to scare me off.

Willing with all my heart that my friend be protected, I neglected in my ignorance to protect myself. My nights were continually tormented. 'This is a very terrible experience, for the victim is afraid to sleep and cannot keep awake indefinitely.' * Still, like a boy scout slogging through the mire, determined to reach the end of the course, I trudged on. And then a very strange thing happened; it may have been sheer coincidence, but I doubt it.

I wanted to sell my cottage in Yorkshire, and one evening about sundown a Mr B. arrived at my door. He said he was interested in viewing the cottage. Although I did not like the look of him I invited him in; he just walked in, out of the blue and into the black, as it were. Dressed entirely in black, with tricorn hat to boot, he looked like a parody of a Dickensian villain. He looked around the cottage, admired it and said he would think over the price I was asking. Then just before he left he fixed me with his gaze. I found I was powerless to take my eyes away. I felt a strange blue ball of light forming above my head and knew that something most unpleasant was happening to me. Try as I might, however, I could not take my eyes off his. I felt a strange force, a triangle, forming from just above my head, my feet, and his feet. I asked Mr B. to leave and he went.

In the morning, glancing out of my back window, I found that a nail had been hammered into the wall and a rope, attached to it, stretched out and secured by a stone to form a triangle. Now I, even I, knew that I was deep into trouble.

Even at this stage, having unwittingly confronted a very powerful Black Magician and, in my ignorance, lost the first

* Dion Fortune, *Psychic Self-Defense*.

round, my pentagram might have protected me. The form of the curse my visitor used will be familiar to anyone knowledgeable in the occult; and, as he was looking about the house, he had of course discovered the only two possible exits to the house, the front door and the back window, and sealed them both off. There was no way in or out of the house without the curse affecting me or anyone entering my home. With sufficient knowledge I could have neutralized the spell, but I had none.

One night, quite unwittingly, while working at the pentagram I managed somehow to blaspheme it. It may have been a word I uttered; it may have been only a thought. But (and there is a witness to this) I was immediately flung backwards across the room and landed soundly with a *crack* against the wall. I remember some voice in my inner mind saying, 'I think we will give you to *Them*'. The use of my legs went immediately; to this day, some four years later, they are not completely sound. My terror, the unspeakable fear of the Unseen, which I felt in the next few weeks is indescribable. When I closed my eyes, figures resembling gargoyles appeared, approached, retreated, approached again, making sleep impossible and reducing me to total exhaustion. My legs contorted into shapes humanly impossible for even the most advanced yogi to imitate and one night they simply wrapped around themselves like two pieces of half-melted liquorice.

A Catholic priest was called in, Irish and none-too-versed in possession or exorcism, and proceeded to half-drown the place and me in a torrent of consecrated water, remarking, 'Thuh Divil hates holy wah-ter'. Even in my state of total panic and physical agony, I remember bursting into laughter at this. He probably assumed it was the Divil Incarnate mocking the powers of Holy 'Mah-ther Charch', as if we were in a scene cut from *The Exorcist*. His performance was most amusing, and of course his 'exorcism' did no good. He only succeeded in goading the entity which was attacking me into further attempts to torment me and break my will, thereby making things worse. He sped from the house and refused to return to it.

But far worse than the physical pain, which was and still is on rare occasions considerable, was the awareness that I was being attacked on a level of the subconscious that I had never before dared to explore. I felt that someone, or something, was literally attempting to scare me to death.

> A sense of fear and oppression is very characteristic of occult attack, and one of the surest signs that herald it. It is extremely rare for an attack to manifest itself out of the blue, as it were. We are not in our normal state of mind, body and circumstance, and then find ourselves suddenly in the midst of an invisible battle. An approaching occult influence casts its shadow on consciousness before it makes its appearance to the non-psychic. The reason for this is that we perceive subconsciously before we realize consciously, and a line of creeping shade indicates the penetrating of the subconscious censor from below upwards.*

In the meantime my friend in London was holding on by a slender thread, a combination of Providence and sheer grit. I had literally to crawl down the stairs from the bedroom to the loo; my physical constitution was at an end. But one day for some reason I was able to pull myself together and walk – looking none too fit to the local inhabitants, I imagine, who already no doubt suspected after a priest had been called in that something funny was going on – to the local coin box and phone my friend. After numerous telephonic delays I managed to reach her and tell her what had occurred, and this, as it happened, was the turning point of the whole situation.

Thomas Aquinas has defined love as the union of two people for the benefit of the other. While the girl herself was under attack, she seemed willing to accept it, as if, as she put it in her letter, she did in fact have a 'self-destructive instinct'. She had nothing of the sort, of course, but the thought had been planted by the attackers in her deep mind. When she learned that I was being attacked as well, her love for me forced her to pull her very powerful self together and fight

* Dion Fortune, ibid.

back. From what scant evidence we have since been able to put together concerning the events of the case (we were neither of us, at the time, in any condition to take clinical notes) it would seem that she was under psychic attack by a very powerful group of Black Magicians or Witches. As an adept she was no easy target, and it seems unlikely that a single person could have created all this havoc. My love and concern for her were gumming up the works, however, and it was decided that I should be put out of the way. In retrospect, it gives me great delight to think that a powerful group of the Left Hand Path could have been foiled by a single Witch and a totally ignorant, if well-meaning, bungler.

My legs still ache occasionally, but otherwise the trouble has cleared up completely and no such attack has ever recurred. To whomever it was who caused all this mess, I can only say that as they wish us well we wish it back to them three times, and add a bit of Vergil: *Amor omnia vincit, et nos cedamus amori.*

I would translate this and hope they take it to heart: Love conquers all things; we too must yield to its power.

The solution

In this case we were dealing with an attack by a group of trained occultists on a Witch. Obviously, in any circumstance where attack or possession is involved that form of prayer or exorcism which works most forcefully on the deep mind will be the most effective. That is why the Lord's Prayer, three versions of which I give on pp. 98–9, is a most potent form of defence against psychic attack. We all grew up hearing it repeatedly, and it affects us all as a conditioned reflex which touches our deepest emotions.

Here now is a form of exorcism used by occultists which has not, to my knowledge, been published previously. Used well and sincerely it is the most powerful defence against psychic attack I know. For various reasons I cannot reveal it in its entirety, but what I shall give of it here may be of enormous help in a drastic situation. I trust that my Brothers in the Craft will understand the need for revealing the essentials of it now. It is, incidentally, one of two Witch rituals I know that cannot possibly cause any harm.

Ritual of the Openings
First, you will require some blessed water and salt. Christian holy water is a combination of water and salt as well, water being a cleanser of spirit and salt a preservative and symbol of the earth, to the Witch a symbol of the Mother Goddess who nourishes and preserves. Water is the great purifier, but unlike salt must first be exorcised. Though many Christian forms of blessing do involve exorcism of the salt, most Witches I know regard this as something of an insult to the Earth Mother. Consecrated water and salt may be obtained from any Roman Catholic or Anglican priest, but you may consecrate it yourself; if the exorcism to be performed involves someone very close to you, this may be even more effective. The exact words used in the act of consecration are unimportant, but the usual formula for salt runs more or less like this:

Salt, beloved representative of the earth and holy symbol of our beloved Mother Goddess: Let all evil fly from hence, and suffer no evil to enter in. So pure are.

A Witch would perform this operation with an athame, or black-handled knife, which has been ritually consecrated. This could be extremely risky if the person performing the operation were a non-initiate, or the knife not of pure steel, or if it had already been used for some other purpose. The right index finger, washed scrupulously clean and rinsed with cold water, will do. Needless to say, before performing such an operation you should have cleansed yourself as thoroughly as possible in mind and body. A bath of lukewarm water with some salt in it is very useful. While rinsing yourself with the water, you may care to repeat the Christian invocation:

Asperges me, Domine, hyssopo, et mundabor; lavabis me et super nivem dealbabor.
(Thou shalt asperge me, O Lord, with hyssop, and I shall be purified; thou shalt cleanse me whiter than snow.)

87

Hyssop is a herb whose twigs were used for sprinkling, rather like the Christian version of aspersion, in ancient Jewish rites. But there may not be time for all this.

> *Water*
> I exorcise thee, O spirit of water. Let all malignity fly from hence, and suffer no evil to enter in. I command the airs of darkness to return to the elements from which they came. So pure be.

Now tip the salt, which may be placed before consecration in a saucer, into the water, saying 'Earth to water'. If you're lucky, you may see a blue light forming above the cup or chalice containing the water (which like everything else used in Ritual Magic should be scrupulously clean); and the salt on hitting the water may create an impression rather like a tiny implosion. If neither of these things happens, don't worry: the important thing is to concentrate on and mean every word you are saying, and to be conscious of the fact that you are calling upon all the preservative powers of earth and water in the universe to aid you. No small matter, this. If your reasons are just, and you yourself are willing to accept the consequences of your actions, you cannot fail.

A Christian form of blessing water and salt, as given by Dom Robert Petitpierre in the pamphlet, *Exorcism,* is as follows:

> *Salt*
> I exorcise you, creature of salt, by the living God, so that you be fit for the healing of mind and body of all who use you. Wherever you are sprinkled may all evil and wicked thoughts depart, all works and deceits of the evil one be driven away, and all unclean spirits be cast out, by him who is ready to judge the living and the dead. Amen.

This strikes me as unnecessarily bossy, but the difference in attitudes between Christian and Witch to created Nature can sometimes be profound. And to reiterate: in performing an exorcism, it is will and intention that count.

Water

Almighty God, Father Eternal, hear our prayers and bless and make holy this creature of water, that it may serve you for the casting out of devils and the driving away of sickness of mind and body. Grant that whatever is sprinkled with this water may be cleansed from all that is foul or harmful. Let no sickness abide there, and cause all the power of the unseen enemy, with his cunning and deceits, to go away.

Through this water dispel all that is contrary to the health and peace of your people, so that, protected by the invocation of your Holy Name, they may be secure against every adversary; through Jesus Christ your Son our Lord. Amen.

As in the previous consecration, the salt is then tipped into the water. In the Witch ritual the water is exorcised first, with the athame plunged into a consecrated chalice; but the water may be exorcised by merely holding a clean cup of tap water between your hands. The form is not important. In Dom Robert's version, however, the following blessing is given to be pronounced at the end:

May this mixing of salt and water be done in the Name of the Father and of the Son and of the Holy Spirit. Amen.

The disturbed person must, at least in the Witch version of the ritual, be naked. (A great deal of rubbish has been written on the subject of why Witches sometimes work in the nude, but more about this later.) Now every entrance of the subject's body is anointed with the consecrated water, or 'sealed off' against any possible form of psychic attack. While this is being done, the right index finger is dipped into the water and pressed gently, in a circular motion, about the entrances. The usual names given to the Witch God and Goddess are Karnayna and Aradia, but a Christian would probably do better to invoke the aid of the Father, the Son and the Holy Ghost.

Sight, I exorcise thee in the Holy Names of —. Let all evil fly from hence, and suffer no evil to enter in.

With this invocation, the eyes are anointed. A Witch would add, 'So mote it be', a Christian, 'Amen': both meanings are similar if not identical. Note also that the parts of the body anointed are named by their functions: thus 'sight' not 'eyes'. The anus is called simply, 'entrance'.

> Smell, I exorcise thee, etc.
> Hearing, I exorcise thee . . .
> Suckle (breasts), I exorcise thee . . .
> Birth (navel), I exorcise thee . . .
> Organ of generation, I exorcise thee . . .
> Entrance, I exorcise thee . . .

While this is being done, both subject and exorcist should try to realize that all the powers of heaven and earth, of water that cleanses and salt that preserves from harm, are being invoked to ward off any evil influence. I have performed this ritual and been told by the subject afterwards that suddenly she felt like a virtual tower of strength; someone across town, who was, I suspect, unconsciously responsible for the disturbance, was immediately taken ill for some days.

At the end of the ceremony, as long as one is not performing it on oneself of course, the exorcist should kiss the disturbed person chastely on the lips and say, 'In perfect love and perfect trust, I give you perfect peace'. Rightly performed, this ritual is proof against any form of psychic attack. It may be repeated as needed. This is the method the disturbed lady in this case used first on herself, then me.

At the end of this ordeal, rather than being scared off occultism forever, I realized that at any cost I wanted to become an occultist. Throughout the entire ghastly experience, which except for occasional pain in my legs seems now like a horrible nightmare, I can remember only one light moment. It occurred during one of the attacks on the lady, before I myself was attacked. She had spent the whole evening raging torrents of abuse and obscenity, trying to kill both herself and me, and had to be physically restrained until towards dawn she passed out. I went to the kitchen, opened the refrigerator and uncorked a bottle of Liebfraumilch. My wits, understandably, were pretty well at an end. I swallowed half the bottle without benefit of glass. Then suddenly, for no reason, flung back my head and began to sing:

This is a luv-v-vly way
To spend an evening . . .

2 The case of the possessed Spiritualist

Catherine is a Christian, married into a strict Roman Catholic family, and a Spiritualist. While I have nothing personally against Spiritualists, I do believe the practice is extremely dangerous when performed by incompetent mediums, just as I feel that all ouija boards should be airlifted away and dumped somewhere far out into the North Sea. My experience of exorcism and of the occult in general has taught me that while discarnate human spirits are relatively easy to attract, they do not always tell the truth and are sometimes not so easy to get rid of; then you are stuck with them. If the discarnate human is not a very pleasant person, you may find yourself in psychic trouble, even severely disturbed. The dead are at least as difficult to live with as the living.

In this case, an inexperienced medium had attracted the discarnate spirit of a woman, whom we shall call Anne, but had been unable to get rid of her at the end of the seance. Anne attached herself psychically to Catherine. Now if anyone's face could be described as literally cherubic, it is Catherine's. Married into a pious (not to say pietistical) family, she took the sacraments regularly, and had one child to whom she was extremely devoted. So it seemed a little odd when she suddenly found herself obsessed with the sudden urge to bash her baby's head against the wall and to hurl invectives at her husband, whom she dearly loved. After a period of great emotional distress, she contacted the woman who had since become my teacher. My teacher went to work on the matter and soon uncovered the problem.

Anne had been a beautiful young woman during the Second World War, married and, like Catherine, the mother of one child. One night, after an air raid, she returned to her apartment to find the entire block devastated by the bombings, except that enough of the building in which she had lived remained for her to discover a bit of her old home left. The bodies of her husband and son had been removed, but instinctively she knew they were both dead. In a state of understandable and forgivable despair, Anne put her head in the oven, turned on the gas and killed herself. In an avalanche of rubbish and with the thought of the two persons she had most loved gone forever, at the utter end of her wits, she committed suicide. To the Witch, who believes in reincarnation, suicide is never a solution to any problem because you'll only wake up somewhere else in another body and in a bigger mess. But I know what Anne felt that night, because in order to free Catherine from possession and give Anne peace, I had to go through the whole experience myself.

My teacher, who is an excellent clairvoyant, having worked out the details of the case, called me up (using the telephone this time), and we went to work immediately. After a modified Witch ritual we summoned the spirit of Anne, my teacher serving, bravely as ever, as medium. Her features changed, not radically but perceptibly, but the voice addressing me was definitely not her own. I found myself, for the first time in my life, holding a conversation with a dead person.

The experience of speaking with someone who has been dead for thirty years is at first a bit startling, not to say frightening, but one becomes accustomed to the situation amazingly quickly. It would have seemed no more, even less, unlikely to a person of the sixteenth century that one could converse with the dead than that I can sit in this room, dial a few digits, and speak with someone in the middle of America. Anyone who has sat in on a genuine seance or experienced a 'ghost scare' will have no trouble in believing what I am saying. Anyone who has not might well recall that, during the period when Anne was alive, 'Fly me to the moon' seemed the wildest of fantasies.

On the first night of exorcism, my teacher and I tried to command the spirit of Anne to depart from Catherine. In this instance, though not always as we shall see in the third case, we were making a big mistake in doing so. It is not always

93

necessary to threaten a spirit to depart from a person. Indeed, I have known of attendant spirits who were positively beneficial, if a little out of their sphere. The spirit may be simply lost, and need a little direction. (This is where I take umbrage with the standard Roman ritual of exorcism.) After a while of this threatening my teacher's face assumed a rather confused look, and the entity left her.

On the second night of the exorcism, my teacher advised me to try reasoning rather than threats. She assumed the spirit of Anne, and the following recorded conversation took place:

'ANNE'. Who . . . who are you?
RICHARD. A friend.
'ANNE'. What d . . . do you want?
RICHARD. To release my friend and to give you peace.
'ANNE'. Peace?
RICHARD. To take you with me, to show you you must die.
'ANNE'. Am I still pretty?
RICHARD. [*touched by this and meaning his reply, because it was true*] Yes. You are still pretty. But for years you have wanted to join your loved ones. Your husband and son. You can do that now. I will help. But you must die.
'ANNE'. Die?
RICHARD. You must stop trying to hold on to what you have already given up. It is frustrating you and causing you to harm other people. I will help you. Hold my hand.
[*At this point the medium extended her hand. It was cold as ice.*]
RICHARD. You need only die once, and then you can rest.
'ANNE'. Rest?
RICHARD. What happened was horrible. It was a long time ago. Now you can rest. But you must leave Catherine. You had your life here; now she has hers. You must get on with yours in a new place. Leave Catherine and go to your husband and son. They are waiting. You must leave her alone, or you will never find the peace you want.

If it sounds like I was addressing a child, that is, in a sense, what I was doing. Anne was a child on what occultists call the etheric plane. She did not in fact know she was dead.

94

Catherine was not present during either exorcism. On the day following the second attempt she came over to my teacher's flat, where, too exhausted to go home, I had spent the night, and told us that on the previous evening she had 'felt something go out of her that [she] hadn't been able to shake for months'. It happened to be about the same time we were working. But she still showed signs of anxiety, so for half an hour my teacher and I performed what exorcists and healers call the laying on of hands. Catherine has persisted, bravely I think, in her study of the occult and she has remained a Spiritualist. She has had a few psychic skirmishes since, but nothing so desperate as in this case.

That was the end of the story for Catherine. But not, due to my foolishness and inexperience, for me and my teacher.

There is a sort of person – if you are reading this book you may be one but, for all our sakes, I hope not – who does not believe in the occult but is fascinated by any kind of novelty. On the intellectual level, you may wonder what electricity really consists of or whether there is life on other planets. On the psychic level, you will be one of those who think that the ouija board is a party game and wonder if Uri Geller really can bend keys. On a lower level you may fantasize what it's like to engage in a sex orgy. You may actually try to join an occult society, mostly out of a strange mixture of scepticism and curiousity. However, if you are accepted, it will most certainly be by a Black group: no society of the Right Hand Path would consider initiating you and no Black congregation would refuse you, especially if you have money, because you are obviously a 'moveable' and your latent psychic powers, as well as your cash, can be used to their ends.

After a long night of exorcising Catherine, one such person arrived. My teacher and I were totally exhausted, she more than I because she had served as medium, always an exhausting role to play in any magical operation. I had never had a chat with a dead person before, having spent the majority of my life thinking it was impossible. My convictions on the subject had suddenly been shaken by the previous evening's activities and, having had maybe four hours of sleep, my intellectual sharpness was not such as to qualify me for the

Cambridge Debating Team.

My teacher was still asleep in the bedroom but I offered our visitor coffee. Sitting over a cup of coffee, half-awake, half resenting the intrusion but feeling that at least I was speaking to another human being still living and breathing, I related the previous night's events. The visitor scoffed. I was a young occultist, and young occultists are notoriously lacking in humility. So my thoughts, such as they were, ran to: 'OK, baby, you've rattled a few tables in your time, but now you're really going to *see* something.' At that same moment, noises started occurring both in the front room, where the exorcism had been performed, and in my teacher's bedroom. I ran to the front room, and before I knew what was happening I was on my hands and knees and then just on my knees with my hands stretched behind my back, head bent forward as if I were about to be beheaded. My head started rattling from side to side, as if bouncing from one wall to another in a space about the size of a gas oven. I smelled, and so did our visitor, the distinct odour of gas. This went on for about five minutes, and apparently I let out a few cries, not for help but of anguish. I came to myself eventually, and our sceptical visitor, understandably anxious to get the hell out of there but nonetheless fascinated, followed me as I ran down the corridor to my teacher's bedroom. She must have been in her bedclothes not five minutes earlier, but now she was sitting, fully dressed, with a glazed look on her face, in the middle of the bedroom floor. She said only, 'Why am I here?' The voice was unmistakable; it was Anne's.

'Because in my ignorance I've called you back,' I said, at this point unsure whom I was addressing, a most horrified-looking dabbler in the occult looming open-mouthed behind me in the doorway. Then I said, 'Go back to your husband. Go back to your son. Go back to where you are happy, and may the peace that passeth understanding be yours forever.'

I was scared out of my wits that I had started the whole thing over again, but somehow those words blurted out and everything calmed down again. What was most curious was that until I began research for this book and consulted the

96

notes we had made on the exorcism, I was unaware that the phrase 'the peace that passeth understanding' had ever passed my lips. As a lapsed Roman Catholic and altar boy of some years' standing, I suppose I must have heard it at some stage, but I could not remember ever speaking it. My teacher recovered from her seizure, I stopped sniffing the aroma of gas, and one dabbler in occultism was cured forever.

Three lessons are to be learned from this case: never indulge in any Spiritualistic activity unless you are sure that the medium is competent not only to summon, but to banish discarnate entities; never try to *force* a discarnate entity to remove itself until you're sure what its motivations and intentions are; and never, never leave the situation in the hands of a young uninitiate until the operation has been both concluded and confirmed. As in the previous case, I came out of this one unharmed because of Providence and the strong presence of a good teacher. As someone once remarked somewhere, God looks after drunks, lunatics and inexperienced occultists.

The Hail Mary, three forms of the Lord's Prayer and the Doxology

In any case of disturbance, mental, moral or physical, these prayers have been known for centuries to have a soothing effect. In a case of genuine psychic disturbance, ie a disturbing entity which has affected a person from outside (obsession) or has in fact invaded the person (possession), they may at first create quite a stir, and the person should be restrained and calmed as gently as possible until a trained exorcist can arrive. First the Lord's Prayer, the most powerful form in English because of the repeated successes it has had over centuries which have added to its potency; then the Latin version, which is more powerful still if your Latin is sure but only likely to inspire scorn in the possessing entity if you pronounce it wrongly. and thirdly my own interpretation of the prayer, which came to me in a dream after I had visited Whitby Abbey. Whitby Abbey is the traditional burial place of Caedmon, so the prayer appears in my book of poems, *Letters Home from Nowhere*, entitled 'Caedmon's Prayer'; it certainly did not come entirely from me. It may or may not work for somebody other than myself: but as they say, any port in a storm.

Before these, however, an invocation to the Virgin Mary, whom Witches call the Mother Goddess but who is in fact one and the same:

> Hail Mary, full of Grace, the Lord is with Thee. Blessed art thou amongst women, and blessed is the fruit of thy womb, Jesus.
> Holy Mary, mother of God, pray for us sinners, now and at the hour of our death. Amen.

Any or all of the following may help to soothe a disturbed individual. If genuine psychic disturbance is present, they may at first start literally a hell of a row, because they are very potent and full of goodwill, which the invading presence is not likely to want to abide very much. They should be recited, half-chanted or whispered lovingly into the person's ear over and over, because however the orthodox churches may regard them they are in fact magical incantations comparable to those used in Witchcraft (in some cases Christian prayers have been stolen quite shamelessly from Witch invocations) and as they are repeated they gain in power, as they take root in the deep mind. But it is well here to paraphrase a remark made by Eliphas Levi, famous French occultist of the previous century, that it is not the ritual itself that brings success in magical operations, but the trained will and intent of the operator. More formulae for relieving a disturbed person will be given in this section; but nothing in heaven, hell or earth is more important towards that end than your perfect love and determination that a human soul be freed, either by you or through you – you are not on an ego trip; if you are, the result may be disaster – from its suffering.

> [After this manner therefore pray ye:] Our Father which art in heaven, Hallowed be thy name.
> Thy kingdom come, Thy will be done in earth, as it is in heaven.

Give us this day our daily bread.

And forgive us our debts, as we forgive our debtors.

And lead us not into temptation, but deliver us from evil; For thine is the kingdom, and the power, and the glory, for ever. Amen. — Matthew 4: 9-13.

Pater noster qui es in caelis, sanctificetur nomen tuum. Adveniat regnum tuum. Fiat voluntas tua, sicut in caelo et in terra. Panem nostrum quotidianum da nobis hodie, et dimitte nobis debita nostra, sicut ut nos dimittimus debitoribus nostris. Et ne nos inducas in tentationem, sed libera nos a malo. Amen.

'Caedmon's Prayer'

Our Father
alive where I am not,
bless your name.

Your Power rule,
your will be done
here
as where I am not.

Give me today
what I need to nourish me
and forgive every malice
as I forgive malice
from others.

And lead me away
from all that looks easy
and can truly destroy me

MALKUTH
HOD
GEBURAH

Let this be.

The three Hebrew words in the last prayer, written by or through me, are from the Kabbalistic Tree of Life and conform roughly, in my mind at least (others will be sure to take umbrage at this), to 'the kingdom, the power, and the glory'. The following is the Doxology, what altar boys call the 'Glory Be'. I shall give first the Latin, then the English version. This prayer is most effective if chanted, recited or whispered repeatedly.

> Gloria Patri et Filio et Spiritui Sancto, sicut erat in principio, et nunc et semper et in saecula saeculorum. Amen.

> Glory be to the Father, and to the Son, and to the Holy Spirit, as it was in the Beginning, is now, and ever shall be. World without end, amen.

It has just occurred to me while typing these prayers that in the extremely unlikely event you should ever need to use them in practice in the case of a person under genuine psychic attack, you might have the book purified and blessed by a priest or Witch of your acquaintance. Before doing so, he or she will doubtless want to read the book. Good.

3 The case of the Edwardian spirit

Therefore if thou wilt have experience: First it becometh thee to know of those things, whether they be hot or colde. And after that note what is the disposition and naturall properties of it, whether it is boldnesse or fearfulnesse, or honestie or barreness.

– Albertus Magnus

One of the strangest, and for me most frightening, cases of possession came to light in an unusual way.

A young man, a Negro and an athelete, was troubled with cramps in his legs. A mutual friend asked if I perhaps could help with this, as the normal training of a White Witch involves healing. When he entered the room I could sense immediately that whatever was wrong with his legs, he was frightened of something. Now even today, with all the publicity rampant on the subject and such serious books as Dr Lyall Watson's *Supernature* crowding the best-seller lists, Witches are still regarded either as curiosities or something to be a little afraid of, so at first I assumed he was nervous of meeting me. An immigrant who had grown up in the ways of Voodoo – a most maligned, misunderstood religion, by the way – might be just that much more wary of a self-professed Witch. But as we spoke it became obvious that his fear was nothing short of stark terror, that it had nothing to do with me, and that he had had it for some time.

It involved, we discovered eventually, the possession of his current (white) girl friend by a discarnate entity. It should be added at this point, because I believe it is relevant to the case, that the young man is a pimp. The girl he was living with had been on the game but was his 'Number 1 Woman' at the time, so she shared his flat with him and was not required to procure. I have sound reasons to believe that he occasionally beat her year-old son and even whipped him occasionally with a bullwhip. Certainly, he beat her habitually. The situation was not one that could be described as suitable material for a script of 'Love thy neighbour' and it was rife with possibilities for psychic disturbance. I was ignorant of all this at the time; had I known all the relevant facts I should probably have acted exactly as I did, only I shouldn't have had to waste so much time getting to the solution. The woman and her son, I heard later, left the young man; though I had absolutely nothing to do with this.

The spirit, whom we shall call Charles, possessing the girl was in a similar situation as Anne in Case 2, but whereas I have every reason to believe that Anne was a lovely person (after all, we did have a few chats together), we had here to deal with a rather unsavoury character. An initial show of force was necessary. Whereas Anne was merely lost and confused, Charles, who had lived in Edwardian times, had been a landed-gentried homosexual alcoholic who occasionally had women because he wanted to make a show of power and domination. To top off this delicious package, he was also a poisoner. Such a discarnate entity was just as likely to feel at home in a domestic situation as I have described as he was to resent Jerry, the young pimp/athlete. Jerry and he had certain qualities in common, but Jerry was ever bit as heterosexual and attractive as Muhammed Ali. Jenny, the girl whose body he was inhabiting, truly loved Jerry, and, as in Case 1, love was gumming up the works. Any psychologist in attendance will realize the significance of the fact that Jenny's brother is homosexual.

The first clue to all of this came about quite accidentally, when, as I was working on Jerry's legs, Jenny walked into the room. There was something, I thought, a bit unusual about the right side of her face. No one's face is perfectly symmetrical, but this had nothing to do with physiognomy. Literally, one side of her face belonged to a different person. We all spoke for a while, and then suddenly, for no earthly reason, she discovered that she had to leave the room.

Later, working on Jerry's legs, and having been told that no medical doctor could find anything wrong with them, I began to consider two possibilities: a lousy bout of nerves, genuine psychic attack, or a mixture of both, the one bringing about and nourishing the other. The idea came to me readily as my own legs had been attacked in precisely the same way (I had been, incidentally, before the incident described in Case 1 and some years previously, the fastest runner at school). But as psychic attack is relatively rare, I put the idea out of my mind and for a few days his legs showed improvement. Then they became worse than ever. As I worked on them for a third time, he remarked about his girl friend, clear out of the blue, 'Man, there's somethin' *on* that woman'.

The Ritual of the Openings, which, as I have said, because it is intended in Perfect Love and Perfect Trust can do no harm even if it's unnecessary, was planned for the following week, once I had assured myself that the girl (when herself) was mentally sound and physically all right. I prepared the room I was using as my temple by casting a circle. I banished the circle just before she was due to arrive – anything, literally *anything*, can happen if a disturbed person is admitted to a properly cast magic circle – but the forces I had invoked left a warm, protective feeling in the room. The girl arrived. She, my wife and I chatted for a while, and then I went back to the temple and prepared things as the girl stripped and got into my wife's dressing gown. And now I suppose is as good a time as any to explain why Witches sometimes work in the nude. It's a bit of a digression, but if you've followed me this far, I'm sure you won't leave.

Some Witches feel that clothing impairs their 'emanations', the powers they raise and send off to do their bidding. In a sense this may be true, but personally I believe it is only psychological. True psychic power acknowledges no physical limitation; it can penetrate walls and travel many miles. My own teacher once did a Witch working from London to middle America, when a cheque I had been promised months earlier by an American lawyer dealing with my father's estate had already been spent in credit and trouble was imminent. For no apparent reason, the cheque arrived within a week. It may have been a coincidence, but the argument was academic to me when I opened that envelope and found I could pay my debts off. The Reverend Neil-Smith has performed successful, if temporary, exorcisms over long distance telephone, once on myself; and much to my surprise, he has allowed me to reproduce in this section the formula he uses. Any power that cannot penetrate a pair of Levis isn't much of a force to be reckoned with. However, there are reasons, even aside from tradition, for working in the nude. The Book of Shadows contains the following passage from the Charge of the Goddess:

> And ye shall be free from slavery;
> And as a sign that ye be truly free,
> Ye shall be naked in your rites.

The 'slavery' referred to in those days was in actual fact physical slavery. The charge of the Goddess was not referring to Women's Lib or streaking but to the more puritanical nature of the Christian church and the repressive nature of medieval authority in general. In these days of popular journalistic send-ups of Witchcraft, 'Ye shall be naked in your rites' may sound like a sales ad for *Playgirl*. It is not. But 'as a sign that ye be truly free' puts us on to one of the really sound reasons why Witches work naked.

First, taking off all your clothes in a group of people removes any number of inhibitions which one develops daily as one grows up: told that Playing Doctor is 'naughty'; forced almost at gunpoint into a confessional to confess to a total stranger that one has 'played with oneself'; and finally, at 'maturity,' dressed to go into the office every day. Not that sexual repression is really the point here: but repression in general, sexual and otherwise, is a block to psychic powers. Being psychic is really only a matter of learning to think in entirely different terms from those to which one has been reduced by 'education'. This is why children, the less 'educated' the better, are natural psychics. When a group of Witches takes off their clothing to work together, many repressions are shed as well. Everyday concerns are shed along with everyday clothing. Anyone so undisciplined and lacking in concentration that he finds himself distracted sexually by the nudity involved shouldn't be working in a circle in the first place. Many Witches, in fact, do not generally work naked unless the specific ritual requires it, but wear special robes, even when their fellow-Witches are Adam-naked. These ceremonial robes are only worn for Witch workings and have the same effect on the wearer as total nudity. They have the same psychological purpose as stripping off; when the wearer puts on his or her robe, he becomes psychologically aware that he is going to work Witchcraft; in other words to tap reservoirs of the Unconscious which most people never use and of which only a few become aware.

In this case, I was going to anoint and 'seal off' a woman's eyes, nostrils, breasts, navel, anus and womb, with consecrated water and that would have been pretty rough through a pair of Levis – at least on my finger. I was fully clothed throughout the ritual, my wife was present in the room, and nothing remotely sexual was intended or occurred.

So much for why Witches work naked, though I expect the popular press hasn't even begun to finish photographing naked bums leaping over log fires. I must add in all honesty that being approached by an attractive nude girl, kissed on the lips and offered a large cup of wine, hearing her say 'Blessed be' and hearing yourself repeat it before having a nice drink, is a most pleasant way to conclude an evening's work of steady concentration. Witchcraft is a religion of joy as well as discipline. Fans of Oliver Cromwell, stop reading here.

As I write, I am wearing a rust-gold coloured sweater and a pair of blue slacks, both of which are disintegrating hourly. But I wouldn't have thought to sit down to write in anything else, though there is no logical reason for this. I just feel very comfortable wearing them; my mind relaxes; I know I am going to write. Anyone who has a favourite sweater, a pet gladiolus or neighbourhood cat, a chair in his study in which he feels most comfortable and experiences slight, if unmentioned, resentment when anybody else sits in it, understands the psychology behind nakedness or robes in

Ritual Magic. One consecrates what one truly loves, and then it is consecrated.

I was wearing this same sweater when the ritual, beginning an hour or so after my own solitary working, began. It started at 10 pm. I remember remarking to my wife before beginning to work with the girl, 'This shouldn't take long'. I have said that three times before beginning a magical operation. On one occasion, the process involved took several months. I will never say it again. The exorcism, if that is in fact what it was, was not concluded until 8 am the following morning.

I performed the Openings ritual, my wife being present, my athame on the altar behind the girl who suddenly gave a violent shudder.

'Richard,' she said as the ritual was concluded.

'Yes?'

'Take that knife away or I'm going to stab you with it.'

'Of course you're not going to stab me with it.'

In fact my athame, whose name is given only to my friends, remained strangely inviolate all through the evening; but the girl did in fact try to strangle me, with a power one wouldn't have suspected in a body that size. But then her energy seemed to drain from her and my wife and I got her onto our chaise longue and covered her with a quilt. She remained in a deep slumber for about fifteen minutes. When she woke up, she asked what had happened. As we were speaking, her features started changing slowly, and she began to revile both me and my wife. Now my ex-wife, who is not a Witch, is nevertheless a very spirited and courageous person and when Charles started in on her he was making the mistake of his death. 'Brandy! Bring me brandy, wench!' he spat at her, and that Welsh, tough-minded look came on to my wife's face. She doesn't like being called a 'wench'. She responded with a flow of invective, in English and Welsh, which would make a sailor armed with a flick-knife turn tail and run, and the subject shut up completely, utterly dumbfounded. Presumably, a servant girl had never spoken to 'him' like that before. Jenny passed out.

Jenny revived shortly, and we then had bouts of apparent schizophrenia such as I hope never to witness again. During one of the lulls I performed the Openings ritual once more. As Jenny was a Christian by baptism I and my wife, who usually is frightened of the occult but rarely panics in an extreme situation, began reciting the Lord's Prayer and the Doxology as she slept. My wife, at one point, gave her tea when she revived from her slumber.

'Jenny *likes* tea,' my wife said.

'Jenny?'

'Likes tea.'

'*Tea???!!!*'

Then followed the hideous, howling laughter to which, by this time, both I and my wife were becoming accustomed. The neighbours weren't, however. The lady upstairs telephoned the police, for which one can't really blame her. All this unearthly yelling and moaning and very earthy haranguing in English and Welsh and, audible through the floor, cries threatening people with knives, combined with the odour of beeswax candles and the lingering scent of frankincense and myrrh, must have conjured up visions of a scene somewhere between Charles Manson and Jack the Ripper.

The police duly arrived and were met at the door by my wife, who said that a friend was visiting who suffered from migraines. Unwisely, but understandably not thinking too clearly at the moment, she allowed them to enter the premises. I had not heard their conversation at the door, involved with administering to Jenny, and, when they entered the temple, I explained that the demi-corpse on the chaise longue was a friend who was visiting and suffering from severe gastric attacks. The officers, England's finest, were no great shakes for intelligence but the surroundings and the conflicting stories definitely did not help. My altar piece is a statue of the Mother Goddess fashioned after a very famous Witch, and she has a moon crescent on her forehead. One of the experts in question decided these were horns. They saw a ritual knife, which I forbade them to touch – oddly enough they obeyed – and a semi-nude girl stretched out on the chaise longue. I could see them already viewing themselves, trying to look cool while explaining all this to ITV and *News of the World*.

'Oy, oy, whot's all 'is, denn,' one of them said. And then,

something which I believe was genuinely providential happened.

Jenny woke up, completely herself, looking as if she had just had eight hours of deep, refreshing sleep. She assured the fuzz that nothing was wrong, that she did in fact suffer from headaches *and* gastric attacks, but was feeling all right now and grateful to have been where somebody could help her. Had Charles taken over at that moment we would have had either two freaked-out heroes in uniform fleeing from the room or all four of us would have been invited to spend the night in jail, including Charles, whom by this time, as you can imagine, I just did not want to know.

As Jenny would make no complaint, there was nothing either policeman could do but look around disgustedly, onto a hot thing here and perhaps a promotion but unable to touch it, and leave the premises. As one of them passed me he muttered under his breath, 'Oy'm naw impressed.'

I answered, aloud, 'Neither am I.'

I left my wife to look after Jenny while going out to phone my teacher for help, also for a taxi; obviously, the ritual could not continue at my flat. We got a cab and went to a friend's place, Charles almost erupting during the journey but, thank the gods, being easily and imperceptibly subdued. By this time my teacher was hard at work not only on Charles but on me, instructing me to *reason* the discarnate entity out of the body.

I began, once we had arrived safely, to speak on a level tone with Charles rather than threaten or command him. I asked him about his life. Intermittently, Jenny went under Charles's influence, passed out, then recovered, asked us what had happened, had some tea and was anointed on the forehead with consecrated water – without, this time, removing her clothes – then began laughing hysterically and attempting to ridicule the whole company, especially myself as 'the bastard who's trying to get rid of me'. By this time, about four in the morning, I was exhausted and frightened but hanging on for dear life, determined never to quit until order had been restored: Charles in his proper place, Jenny in hers. Before undertaking an exorcism or battling a psychic attack, you are a fool not to consider the possibility that you might be beaten. Once you are in it, you are a fool to think that you can. In this case a show of force had been necessary initially, because Charles was not the sort of person to speak seriously to anyone of whom he wasn't a little afraid. But now my teacher, the Feminine Principle in the sense of a responding, loving mother, took over and guided my line of approach. Charles suddenly became confused, as he no doubt would have during the time he inhabited his body, by genuine affection and concern.

'Why haven't they buried me?' he asked, like a child inquiring why there are no lights on the tree.

'But they have. You just don't know how long you've been dead.'

'Dead?'

'Yes, Charles. Dead.'

About 8 am, while speaking with Jenny/Charles, I began to feel a strange white light just behind my right shoulder. Occultists know that at the moment of physical death – death being regarded as nothing more than a change in one's state of awareness – a spirit guardian, one's 'Guardian Angel', comes to welcome the spirit and to be its guide in a totally strange environment. The environment is not really that strange, because, as Dion Fortune remarked, you go there every night in your dreams. But if you are frightened, or have left unfinished business in your earthly life, or are deeply attached to your body – a good argument for cremation, by the way, because immolation of the corpse makes a haunting just that much more difficult – you may become a confused, unfortunate wanderer like Anne or Charles. The white light was undoubtedly Charles's guardian. I was not the only one to experience it, and one person in the room actually saw it quite clearly. Jenny rose unsteadily to her feet, and taking her by both hands I began, walking backwards, to lead her towards the place I could feel as the source of the light.

'That is your Guardian. Go to him,' I said. I still don't know why.

'Guardian?'

'He will teach you. He knows what you need.'

At this point a tangible presence left the room. Three of us now, besides Jenny, who had passed out at my feet, felt it leaving. We all had some tea, mine laced, deservedly I think, with a good belt of rum; after all, I had to get dressed up and be at work in a couple of hours. My own exhaustion and the fear I had felt all along having passed, I suddenly realized what I'd been through. The room was quiet. Jenny went home to bed, and so did my wife. To the best of my knowledge, Jenny has had no such trouble since.

My wife by the way had come up with the most potent formula for exorcism in this case. Although there were other complications between the two people to be faced in the future, my wife, when the entity seemed to be gaining complete control, simply held Jenny's hand and repeated, 'You are Jenny. Jenny loves Jerry.'

Obviously, this was no picnic. No exorcism is an ego trip or an occasion for a strawberry festival. Two lessons were learned here: first, no exorcism should be undertaken alone or in a place where there is the remotest possibility that the operation may be disturbed. Second, one must never quit or leave the patient unattended until a trained exorcist is certain that the ritual has been concluded successfully. The true exorcist does not say, 'Okay, we got rid of most of the demons but we're pretty bushed so let's knock off and start again tomorrow. So far, we know this guy won't commit adultery, or covet his neighbour's goods, or be gluttonous, or any of that stuff. Now let's hit the hay.' The disturbed person may, and in one case did, just meander home and murder his wife.

4 The case of the Black Witch

'A foolish consistency is the hobgoblin of little minds.'

— Emerson

'What did you say? A great man? Every time I look I see only one who acts out his own ideal.'

— Nietzsche, *Beyond Good and Evil*

Black magic is opposed to White magic, but that is not to say they have nothing in common. The day and the night are opposed, as are man and woman; but they perennially pursue one another, and without the one the other could not exist. No White Witch of my acquaintance has not found himself in the position, at one time or another, of having to be cruel only to be kind. White Witches refer to members of Black covens as Brothers of the Left Hand Path, and when they say Brothers they mean it – brothers can quarrel too, you know.

In any situation where one is proposing to affect another's mind – psychiatrically, by sorcery, or by using plain old kitchen psychology – a tremendous moral responsibility is involved. The exorcist, who is a sort of a magician whether he cares to admit it or not, must examine his motives very carefully. Magic deals with the subconscious in very much the same manner as psychiatry, only more directly and more effectively. If the object in mind is destruction, the result may be psychic attack. If one means to do White working, one must still consider the consequences of the outcome. There is also the very pertinent question of whether anyone has the right to invade another's mind without the other's knowledge or consent. I believe that in some cases, if one knows what one is doing and is willing to bear the consequences, one has. Only one must do it, as the Christians phrase it, with one's whole heart, whole soul, whole mind, whole body. In other words, in order to work to someone else's benefit one must first of all believe in oneself – and be worthy of that belief.

Any discussion of the difference between White and Black Witchcraft involves the question of what theologians call 'positive evil'. To the Christian, even to theologians of the stature of Augustine or Aquinas, this problem is, to put it mildly, a bit of a sticky wicket. No one of them has ever solved it. Put briefly, it amounts to this: if God is all-powerful, all-knowing and all-good, the Creator and Governor of all that exists, then how can evil *be*? An effect, Aristotle tells us, must be similar to the cause. Thomas Aquinas, who was breast-fed on Aristotle, never managed to argue his way out of the fact that if God is all-good and the cause, 'prime mover', of the universe, then evil cannot exist. But as Chesterton observed, to verify the existence of evil all one need do is walk out into the street.

The Christian 'answer' is that evil in a sense does *not* exist, which first of all makes you wonder what we need their church for in the first place, and secondly reminds you of the sort of conversation you could expect from Marshall McLuhan about half an hour after he'd o.d.'d on acid. What we need their church for in the first place is easily explainable: they need us, we make them money. The question of evil's existence in the 'best of all possible worlds' is a bit more difficult.

Dostoevsky wrestled with, even physically suffered over, this question all his life, so I do not propose to cope with it myself just here and now. If you are of an impish nature, you may quote some of the more pertinent passages of his work to the local vicar. I personally am of the belief that 'good' and 'bad' are relative and totally inadequate terms to define the situation in which we find ourselves as human beings. Ultimately we are all *affirming*, whether we choose to admit it or not. The White Witch says 'Yes'; the Black Witch says 'No'; in the end they all add up to a kind of 'YESNO' that we cannot, at this stage of our evolution, properly define. And perhaps this is God.

When 'YESNO' gets a little out of line, we have psychic

disturbance. 'YESNO', interpreted as 'I am who am' or Yahweh, cannot be permanently disturbed or even very much bothered at all, but on our level of existence we may feel a certain tremor when Black magic is being performed. This was what happened in the case I shall describe in a moment. I may however add in passing that those 'solid citizens' who disagree that the mind ought to be tampered with without the patient's knowledge ought to examine their own lives and see how often they buy a product just because the jingle composed to advertize it is ringing imperceptibly in their ears; how many prescriptions they have swallowed without bothering to enquire as to the contents; or how much tax money they spend yearly to support the 'treatment' being given by electric shock, which poses as a form of therapy but is in fact a sort of psychic euthanasia.*

I remember raising havoc in religion class once as a kid, when the Reverend Brother was explaining how God could do anything. I asked if he could sin. The Reverend brother replied that of course God couldn't sin, whereupon I replied that if he couldn't sin he couldn't do anything he wanted, could he? The Reverend Brother said, in effect, shut up. But I was honestly curious, as children are. I couldn't get around the problem and wondered about it constantly, even at home, or on the playground. I discussed it with some of my classmates, thereby ruining a few promising clerical careers. I kept bringing it up in religion class. Finally the Reverend Brother gave up and they sent in a full-fledged priest, trying to pull rank. I didn't see the point of all this until much later, when I had left the church and was myself a lecturer at the University of Kansas. I enjoyed shaking up my students with such questions as:

'Are you alive?'

'Yeah.'

'How do you know? Have you ever been dead?'

One day when the Comparative Literature class was flagging the old question came into my mind, so I brought it up. In discussing it, we realized that the Latin for sin, *peccatum*,

* Joan Grant, on hearing me use this phrase about shock therapy, remarked: 'It is worse. It is psychic torture.'

really only meant 'mistake', just as 'repent' comes from *re* (again) and *pensare* (to think), so that 'to repent' only means, etymologically, 'to re-think'. How could the Summit of Existence, 'I am who am', make a mistake? He 'makes' all right, as an active principle sustaining all that exists, but more to the point, He *Is*. The person who, in the following case, was exorcised came very quickly and dramatically to realize this.

In *The Exorcist And The Possessed,* Neil-Smith describes an exorcism he performed on a Black Witch who had asked for help.

During the exorcism, Neil-Smith put his hands on the subject's head, at which point she had a violent physical reaction, almost an epileptic fit. (Epilepsy, by the way, used to be considered a form of possession, and sometimes the physical symptoms are similar.) She picked herself up from the floor in something resembling a trance state and began to amble towards the main doorway of St Saviour's Church, of which Neil is pastor and which has seen a few exorcisms in its time. He was following at a distance to see she did herself no harm. But she took a wrong turn and arrived in the Lady Chapel, dedicated to the Blessed Virgin, whom Witches call the Goddess. She proceeded to attack the statue, attempting to dash it to bits. When Neil restrained her she burst into hysterical tears, renounced the Left Hand Path, and Neil felt something depart from her aura at that moment. A few moments earlier, when she had begun to feel the effect of the exorcism, she had pushed his hands away from her head and it suddenly came into his mind to reach her hands out into the form of a Christian cross. This is what precipitated the crisis. I asked him several years ago what had prompted him to do this and he replied, 'I think it was inspiration'.

Discussing the case some years later, compiling material for this book, I asked him again.

'Oh, I dunno,' he said, relaxing in his study with a glass of sherry. He had performed perhaps 1,000 exorcisms since. He'd forgotten. Even exorcists are human.

Black magic has been described as finding yourself trapped on a merry-go-round that suddenly shifts, at enormously high speed, from the right to the left. If you can manage to find the

114

ledge and leap off it, you will find yourself on the ground but a little shaken to say the very least, and it will be some time before you recover your equilibrium or any sense of the direction you were heading for in the first place. If the damage due to the fall was severe, you will never be quite the same again. That was not the case with this lady, whose Christian and Witch names are known to both Neil and myself, but which I do not propose to reveal.

The exorcisms I have cited here were all successful. This is not to suggest that all, or even most exorcisms have happy outcomes. George Alexander, a magician who makes magical weapons and talismans to earn his living, told me once of a woman whom a group was attempting to exorcise once every week. Invited along to help, he began to realize very early in the ceremony that the woman did not *want* to be exorcised. An elderly widow, she lived alone and she coveted all the attention the weekly exorcisms brought her. Even the entity obsessing her was a form of company she would miss, and once they had got rid of it, she would subconsciously call it back again. Another case in which I was involved concerned a woman whose husband was deceased and kept returning on the anniversary of his death and other occasions, asking her to join him. Personally, she and I both feel with all the wisdom of hindsight that all the 'hauntings' were purely subjective. The lady has a powerful will of her own and when she decided for herself that these events would stop, they did. She has had no trouble since I have known her, which is over a year. No exorcism was attempted. As is usually the case, none was required.

Then, too, in a case where genuine psychic disturbance is present, real humour, as opposed to cynical, despairing laughter such as convulsed poor Charles in Case 3, can be very therapeutic. I know of one occasion in which an attacking entity was literally laughed out of the room. During the time when I was under psychic attack, I stayed for a while at a friend's flat just off Baker Street. I decided to take an impromptu vacation to Brighton to absorb some sun and recover my equilibrium, and my friend returned to his flat. On the first night he spent there, just before dozing off to sleep, he began to sense the unearthly chilliness that often heralds a psychic attack and distinctly heard the sound of what occultists call the astral bell – I shall describe this later. Terrified as he was, the worst was yet to come: although no visible presence was with him, he suddenly received a violent kick in the stomach. Frightened beyond fright and remembering what I had told him about the attacks I was undergoing, he realized that a mistake had been made by whomever was attacking me, and the funny side of the situation overwhelmed him, so that he burst into laughter. 'Oh, *him*,' he addressed whatever was in the room. 'You've got the bloody wrong address. He's off in Brighton.' He literally started rolling around the bed with laughter, and the chilliness in the room departed immediately. Somebody, somewhere, that night, had the devil to pay.

5   Under psychic attack

The nature of the attack

Some of the aspects of the probable nature of possession or psychic attack have already been mentioned in Case 1. The first symptom that something is wrong is the general sense of oppression, constant bouts of depression for no reason. Recurrent nightmares are quite common. But in the case of the actual manifestation of an entity, visible or otherwise, the unmistakable warning that something is about to happen is an indescribable chilliness in the air, the sort that is sometimes experienced in certain spots in haunted houses. There is no way to describe this sensation to one who has not experienced it, but 'bone-chilling' is as good a way as any to try. One's immediate reaction to this utterly piercing coldness is fear, but after a few experiences one comes to recognize it as a blessing in disguise; at least the invading entity has been forced to announce that something is about to happen, and if 'it' could operate without creating this frosty herald of impending attack I am certain that it would so so. You have time to get ready for the unexpected.

On the occasion I mentioned in Case 3 when it became impossible to continue the exorcism at my home and I had to go out to phone for a taxi to take the possessed person to the house of a friend, as I approached the phone box I was aware of this chill. Although half a mile away from my apartment (my wife was looking after the disturbed person) I knew something was happening back at the flat. I got the telephoning business over with as soon as possible and as it turned out at the precise moment I felt the chill the patient had been overwhelmed with the desire to lock me out of the house.

117

Here is an actual account by someone under attack at the time, of what the general sensation is like. She cannot remember writing it.

> An icy stillness seemed to creep over the room. It felt as if suddenly a powerful blow had been dealt to the stomach, and the chair in the corner of the room seemed to be going quite mad. Dancing almost, but moving about certainly.
>
> Can you feel colour? The hue of cold seemed to pervade the room. The coldness departed as mysteriously as it had come, but some minutes later it returned, but it felt differently [sic], an inquiring atmosphere, rather than icy stillness. The coldness passed through the house and then departed for the night.
>
> The coldness is difficult to describe, because it is not one that comes of snow or wind, but rather of a temperateless [sic] presence that seems to take hold of that abstract part of yourself. The experience is always of the unexplainable, relying on feel, atmosphere and instinct. This is sometimes the only 'physical' evidence one has of psychic attack; more often the whole operation is based on mental attitude. Here 'feel' and 'instinct' play an even bigger part and it is of course even more difficult to explain or rationalize – even to yourself.
>
> 19 December 1972

If you have experienced this degree of disturbance, it is time to seek help. Notice too that the account bears out what I have said about the primary phases of psychic attack being mental and therefore hard to cope with or even believe.

Another warning of imminent attack is the astral bell, which I have mentioned in connection with my own psychic disturbance of some years ago, when the attacker had misfired and sent an attack on a friend of mine who distinctly heard the tone of a bell before the chilly presence began to be felt in the room. This extremely disturbing sound may range in tone from anything like a resonant bell, a crystal goblet being struck with the fingernail, to a noise resembling a rifle crack. The possessed person in Case 1 distinctly heard – as did I – the baying of a hound outside her window, which we deemed unusual because she lived on the second floor and had no balcony. The baying faded into the distance and, this having occurred about midnight, we assumed an attack was imminent. We were correct.

These two occurrences, disturbing as they may be at first, serve, quite unintentionally I am sure on the part of the attacker, a positive purpose: they give you time to contact an exorcist, or to prepare to defend yourself.

Of course in some cases, particularly when one occultist is attacking another, the forms which the attack take may be more immediately recognizable and violent. Maxine Sanders, Witch Queen, who runs her famous coven from Notting Hill Gate, had a narrow escape from death once when her daughter, Maya, called her out of the way just in time to escape a huge iron talisman, firmly attached to a beam over a doorway, crashing to the floor for no explainable reason. The effect on Maxine's skull would have been at the very least a severe brain concussion. For this and other reasons, Maxine decided that someone was attacking her. Picking a psychic battle with a Witch as powerful as Maxine is like taking a slug at Joe Bugner in a pub. Once she had determined, by divination, who was attacking her, the matter was soon settled to everyone's satisfaction except the attacker's, who has been strangely quiet lately. If you awaken one day to find that all your hair has fallen out, it would be wise to assume that you are under a severe attack of an unusually powerful nature, and immediately to seek the aid of a Witch or Christian exorcist (as well as a firm dealing in hair transplants). But such occasions are rare.

Under normal circumstances, if you feel recurrent, consistent and unexplainable oppression such as I have described, you are well advised to see a physician and, if he so advises, a psychiatrist. Failing all else, see an exorcist.

What to do
The hardest advice first: Don't panic. Occurrences of genuine

possession are rare, but they do happen, and the last thing needed in such a situation is an *un*possessed fruitcake jumping around confusing everything and everybody, which is just the sort of situation the attacking entity is trying to create. Calm down; whatever is happening, people have gone through worse and lived to talk – even write – about it. Calm the disturbed person as best you can: put on some soothing music perhaps. Remember your Shakespeare: the mad King Lear was comforted by music, as prescribed by a physician; so was the magician, Prospero, who prescribed it for himself. A calm atmosphere, blue or white candles absorbing and neutralizing the evil presence in the room – consecrated if possible with holy oil – comfortable warmth, and above all an atmosphere of positive love are what is required until an exorcist can arrive. With regard to the latter, if you sense or suspect some secret resentment in yourself towards a disturbed person, leave the premises immediately and distract your mind as best you can. See a *Carry On* film, or something. Detach yourself from the patient mentally and physically because, through no fault of your own, you may be causing the disturbance or abetting it. Don't feel guilty; you probably have no reason to. But out of mercy and love don't hang around if you feel, for any reason, that you are doing more harm than good.

If consecrated water is available, anoint the patient's forehead in the sign of the cross of Christ or that of Malkuth, while reciting the doxology. If the person is Christian, you might find the Christian sign of the cross more effective. If he is of some other religion, the sign of Malkuth might be better: Witches use it constantly, and it is older than the Christian symbol. Mixing traditions is not of importance here: only results. We need a calm, soothing place to rest. In a case of genuine possession, applying holy water to the forehead may cause a violent reaction in the subject: again, don't panic. A violent reaction from a possessing entity only means that you are gaining control of the situation and that it, not you, is losing energy.

Do what you can, before the exorcist or physician arrives, to make yourself comfortable and to retain your strength. You will need it. But under no conditions give the person alcohol,

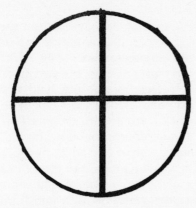

The sign of Malkuth

or any form of drug, until the condition has been analysed by a qualified physican or exorcist, preferably both. Some drugs not only weaken but destroy the aura. Giving a truly psychically disturbed person LSD or any other form of mind-boggling drug might give the attacking entity just the entrance it needed. Alcohol acts as a depressant; it says to the mind, 'It's easy; give in; let me take over; it will be easier'. That is *not* what we want.

I once watched someone who may or may not have been possessed going into a fit and being attended by a person who loved her. The situation was not critical, and one should never interfere, in such instances, unless specifically asked, so I did nothing but look on as the chill in the room came and went. The person alternately became violent and then passed out. Upon awakening, she immediately asked for a drink. The person attending objected, but always gave in and as soon as the subject had absorbed the alcohol into her system, the demon, even if it was only the demon drink, started ranting and raving again. I began to notice a regularity in the time it took between the disturbed woman having a drink and the recurring eruptions.

'Sixty seconds,' I said as our friend handed a gin and tonic to the subject.

I was only a few seconds off. The ranting and raving started in very nearly a minute; I timed it. In this situation there was no point in trying to tell anybody what ought to be done, because the emotional complications would have been

121

incalculably complex and the attack was not severe. But I'm telling *you:* if you have reason to believe that someone is under psychic attack, do not give him alcohol. You might need a few belts yourself to steady your nerves, but be careful: there are demons who actually feed on alcohol, and two possessed drunks at this stage is not a terribly good idea.

In the case I have just mentioned nothing serious happened, but the cost in a night's consumption of gin and Canadian Club must have been enough to give anybody the spooks.

What to do then? As I advised at the outset, stay calm and remember that genuine cases of possession are rare. If one exists, also remain calm; remember that something Unseen is trying to frighten you, so expect the unexpected and be careful though not paranoid. You have all the positive forces of earth, water, air and fire, every positive force in the universe, on your side; not an inconsiderable advantage. If there is some delay in the exorcist arriving, continue your life as usual. The burden of proof is all on the attacker. The keywords are presence of mind, selfless love, unshakeable courage and goodwill.

If in need of an exorcist, call the organization Release or 01 222 9011, which is an Anglican church information centre which will put you in touch with a competent person. *Alternative London* lists the telephone number of the Reverend Neil-Smith. The telephone number of Release is 01 289 1123. In an emergency, for Release call 01 603 8654. For Witch help, 01 229 6861.

A formula for exorcism

The Reverend Christopher Neil-Smith has accomplished exorcism over long-distance telephone. In writing a book of this nature, ie dwelling continually on the subject, one is likely to suffer some psychic disturbance. I was warned of this by Françoise Strachan, who experienced occasional distress while writing *Casting Out the Devils,* a book which remains the classic authority on the actual facts of exorcism for laymen. On one occasion I telephoned Neil and asked for his blessing. I'd had a hard day's work, felt anxious about revealing some of the processes of exorcism contained in this book, and was too exhausted to put up with any form of anxiety whatever. Neil has given me permission to publish his short formula for exorcism, which may be of use in an emergency. Remember, however, and I cannot say this too often, that will and intention, not formulae, are what counts, and that Neil is a natural psychic and highly experienced exorcist. I received this blessing some few minutes before I wrote this.

O God, unconquered Might, who keepeth all that are against Thee, who by His death has destroyed death and overcome the prince of death, BEAT DOWN SATAN under our feet, and CAUSE this evil force to depart and never more hold tyranny over your soul; and give place to Christ.

When pronounced by Neil, as I have personal reason to testify, this is a most potent psychic cleanser.

Passing the Hands
This passage is quoted directly from the Book of Shadows. I have had more than second thoughts about giving it here, because anyone inexperienced in exorcism would be very foolish to try it. On one occasion I saw one of the most powerful magicians in Europe drained, if only for a few moments, after performing this ritual. She had absorbed a great deal of hostile energy and had to rest awhile before it completely left her. It would be mad for an inexperienced magician to take a hostile force into himself, because he might find he's stuck with it, like the priest in *The Exorcist* who only succeeded in exorcising the demon from a little girl by taking it upon himself and then abruptly committed suicide. This actually happened to a famous pop star who knew enough about magic to release a friend of his from possession and shortly thereafter threw himself in front of a train. But no book on exorcism would be complete without this ritual being quoted, and for the benefit of those initiates who can use it and for the interest of everyone, I give it here. For the dabblers in the audience who might try it out of curiosity I can only say: No.

123

Commence by making passes from the soles of the feet to the crown of the patient's head. This will neutralize the effects of the Evil Eye, etc. Place the hands palms down upon the top of the patient's brain, until you feel the current tingling in the outstretched fingers. Proceed to make passes from the summit of the head downwards alongside the face, along the outstretched arms to the fingertips. Complete the treatment by making further passes down the spine from the top of the vertical column and continuing them to the extremities, then wave the hands sideways with a quick jerk to throw off and dissipate the unhealthy magnetism drawn by this process from the system of the patient. All who undergo this treatment will testify to its singular efficacy.

From the exorcist's point of view, the most important thing to remember is that if he ignores or does not concentrate sufficiently on dissipating rather than absorbing the 'unhealthy magnetism', he may find him*self* in a hell of a fix.

Psalms of defence

I have quoted here three psalms which may prove to be of use in case of psychic attack. If you are not a trained exorcist, do not commence by bellowing them over the patient as if you saw yourself as Charlton Heston parting the sea. Recite them, over and over if need be, with fervour and conviction until help arrives. They may be alternated with the Doxology and the Lord's Prayer.

Psalm 57
Be merciful unto me, O God, be merciful unto me: for my soul trusteth in thee: yea, in the shadow of thy wings will I make my refuge, until these calamities be overpast.

I will cry unto God most high; unto God that performeth all things for me.

He shall send from heaven, and save me from the reproach of him that would swallow me up. Selah.* God shall send forth his mercy and his truth.

---

* pronounced 'Say-lah'.

My soul is among lions; and I lie even among them that are set on fire, even the sons of men, whose teeth are spears and arrows, and their tongues a sharp sword.

Be thou exalted, O God, above the heavens; let thy glory be above all the earth.

They have prepared a net for my steps; my soul is bowed down; they have digged a pit before me, into the midst whereof they are fallen *themselves*. Selah.

My heart is fixed, O God, my heart is fixed: I will sing and give praise.

Awake up, my glory; awake, psaltery and harp: I *myself* will awake early.

I will praise thee, O Lord, among the people: I will sing unto thee among the nations.

For thy mercy *is* great unto the heavens, and thy truth unto the clouds.

Be thou exalted, O God, above the heavens: *let* thy glory *be* above all the earth.

Psalm 23
The LORD *is* my shepherd; I shall not want.

He maketh me to lie down in green pastures: he leadeth me beside the still waters.

He restoreth my soul: he leadeth me in the paths of righteousness for his name's sake.

Yea, though I walk through the valley of the shadow of death, I will fear no evil: for thou *art* with me; thy rod and thy staff they comfort me.

Thou preparest a table before me in the presence of mine enemies: thou anointest my head with oil; my cup runneth over.

Surely goodness and mercy shall follow me all the days of my life: and I will dwell in the house of the LORD forever.

This, perhaps the most well-known of the psalms, has a positive and soothing effect whether one is experiencing any disturbance or not. 'The valley of the shadow of death' has,

however, been interpreted by some as a direct reference to the
Evil Eye.

Psalm 59

Deliver me from mine enemies, O my God: defend me
from them that rise up against me.

Deliver me from the workers of iniquity, and save me
from bloody men.

For lo, they lie in wait for my soul: the mighty are
gathered against me; not for my transgression, nor for
my sin, O LORD.

They run and prepare themselves without my fault:
awake to help me, and behold.

Thou therefore, O LORD God of hosts, the God of
Israel, awake to visit all the heathen : be not merciful to
any wicked transgressors. Selah.

They return at evening: they make a noise like a dog,*
and go round about the city.

Behold, they belch out with their mouth: swords are in
their lips: for who *say they,* doth hear?

But thou, O LORD, shall laugh at them; thou shalt have
all the heathen in derision.

Because of his strength will I wait upon thee; for God
is my defence.

The God of my mercy shall prevent me: God shall let
me see my desire upon my enemies.

Slay them not, lest my people forget: scatter them by
thy power; and bring them down, O Lord our shield.

For the sin of their mouth *and* the words of their lips let
them even be taken in their pride; and for cursing and
lying which they speak.

Consume *them* in wrath, consume *them,* that they *may*
not *be:* and let them know that God ruleth in Jacob unto
the ends of the earth. Selah.

And at evening let them return: *and* let them make a
noise like a dog, and go round about the city.

Let them wander up and down for meat, and grudge if
they be not satisfied.

* Cf Case 1.

*But I will sing of thy power; yea, I will sing aloud of thy mercy in the morning: for thou hast been my defence and refuge in the day of my trouble.

Unto thee, O my strength, will I sing: for God *is* my defence, *and* the God of my mercy.

Historically (the word should really be in quotation marks) this psalm is said to have been composed by David when Saul sent assassins to surround his home. But in the case of psychic attack it is singularly appropriate.

There are many other prayers in the Book of Psalms which are powerful against the effects of psychic attack; Psalm 46 is very apt, for example. But read through the entire prayer before you start chanting it aloud; just in the middle you may find yourself reciting a very sincere and potent curse.

Indeed, Psalm 59 gives some hint of the often virulent nature of these prayers, which are really magical invocations. In a case of psychic disturbance, when you say the attack is 'not for my transgression, nor for my sin,' you'd better know you mean it.

Rituale Romanum
The Roman Catholic formula of exorcism, which is very powerful, is too lengthy to be quoted here in full and in any case should only be performed by two Roman Catholic priests at the very least, one of whom is an experienced exorcist. One passage of interest, however, is as follows:

Praecipio tibi, quicumque es, spiritus immunde, et omnibus sociis tuis hunc dei famulum obsidentibus, ut per mysteria Incarnationis, Passionis, Resurrectionis et Ascenscionis Domini Nostri Jesu Christi, per missionem Spiritus Sancti, et per adventum eiusdem Domini nostri ad judicium dicas mihi nomen tuum, diem, et horam exitus tui cum aliquo signo; et ut mihi Dei ministro, licet indigno, prorsus in omnibus obedias; neque hanc

* Personally, I'd suggest you omit these latter two verses. They express an aggressive attitude whereas, in the hands of the untrained, *defence* is the keynote.

127

creaturam Dei, vel circum stantes, aut eorum bona ullo modo offendas.

Translated in my own version and not that of the actual Roman ritual, which as I have said would be risky in the extreme for anyone but an ordained Catholic priest to try, this means:

> I command you, O unclean spirit, whoever you are, and all your companion spirits who are afflicting this servant of God, to reveal to me your name, your lord, and the hour of your departure, by some sign; I command you through the mysteries of the Incarnation, the Passion, Resurrection and Ascension of our Lord Jesus Christ, by the power of the Holy Spirit, and by the coming of that same our Lord to the final judgement, that you obey me, a minister of God, however unworthy, in all things, and that you do no harm to this creature of God, nor to anyone here present or their possessions, in any way.

Were I to use this ritual invocation this is how I would phrase it in my own words; but I would not use it because I am not a Catholic priest.

A traditional prayer
This prayer should be used after the exorcism has been concluded and the patient anointed with oil by an ordained minister. It has the effect of sealing off the disturbed person from outside interference, rather than expelling a disturbing entity. It bears a curious resemblance to a similar chant recited by the Navajo Indians.* In occultist terms, its purpose

* I walk with beauty
before me
I walk with beauty
behind me
I walk with beauty
below me

I walk with beauty
above me
I walk with beauty
all around me.

The full text of this American Indian chant is an excellent morning invocation and is given on p. 138.

128

is to reinforce the protective powers of the aura; it is normally performed along with the Passing of Hands.

> The Lord GOD be within you to strengthen you; outside you to preserve you; over you to shelter you; beneath you to support you; before you to guide you; behind you to steady you; around you to secure you.

This prayer is a slight variation on what is known as St Patrick's Breastplate. A similar version has been traced to Egypt.

A positive and soothing prayer 'For Peace and Deliverance from our Enemies' is given in the *Book of Common Prayer,* and may be used at morning or evening or both. It is essential to reiterate, however relentlessly, that no prayer is a matter of *formulae*. Never simply jabber a prayer. It only weakens its efficacy, by making the words commonplace and eventually meaningless to your deep mind.

> O Almighty God, who art a tower of defence unto thy servants against the face of their enemies; We yield thee praise and thanksgiving for our deliverance from those great and apparent dangers wherewith we were compassed: We acknowledge it thy goodness that we were not delivered over as a prey unto them; beseeching thee still to continue such thy mercies towards us, that all the world may know that thou art our Saviour and mighty Deliverer; through Jesus Christ our Lord. Amen.

Guilt and self-exorcism
'L'enfer, c'est nous-même.'

Françoise Strachan has spoken of the 'absolute necessity' of exorcising oneself. It is probably true that the most difficult thing to exorcise in oneself is one's own sense of guilt. The 'It's-All-My-Fault' syndrome occurs often in victims of psychic attack and leads to the 'I-Deserve-What-I-Get' state of mind that is the delight of every psychic attacker, from the stupidest nagging housewife to the most highly developed Black Magician. If the person under attack can be made to

129

despise himself, the job is three-quarters done. In fact, a successful attack is almost assured and even more deliciously so in the eyes of the attacker because he has led his victim into a mental trap in which he is *self*-destructive, so that no amount of exorcism can stop it. No one can be exorcised if he does not want to be.* Medical doctors speak of some patients as 'having lost the will to live'. When a willing victim comes under competent psychic attack, his state is much worse: he feels he has lost the *right* to live and like a mesmerized virgin walking towards Dracula he resigns himself to his doom. One victim of psychic attack said to me, 'Sometimes I get these feelings that I'm going to die; but I get up some mornings anyway and think, OK, so I'm going to die. Long before this trouble started. But this kind of dying means something far, far worse.' There really are fates worse than death.

I know a woman who, the last time I saw her, was a nervous wreck. She had inflicted a good deal of needless pain on someone whose life she had partially, but irreparably, shattered. For professional reasons she occasionally had to come into contact with this person. Usually she just went stone-cold, but on more than one occasion she actually fled the room. She described herself as frightened of this person, but in fact she was frightened of the realization that she had earned the right to be frightened of him, so to speak. Not strong enough to endure this sort of pain (it is interesting that she could not bear the slightest physical pain, either), she was protecting herself by pretending the person she had hurt didn't exist – or at any rate, didn't matter. The mere sight of this person was hateful to her – as Anouilh observed, 'One always hates what one wrongs'. Guilt was unthinkable, unbearable. She had at one time been in love with the man in question, who had behaved badly to her on several occasions. Not quite sure that she had sufficient reason to despise a person in whom she must have seen something good, she

* In my opinion it is not possible to exorcise anyone against his will. Christopher Neil-Smith disagrees and is obviously more experienced than I am, but I think that although it may be possible temporarily to disorientate a possessing spirit and drive it from its lodge, the individual must co-operate or find himself possessed again.

130

behaved even more badly to him in order to convince herself that she ought to be frightened of him. If I may sound like R.D. Laing for a moment, the train of her reasoning was:

> I don't know what to do because I love him but I think I'm frightened of the way he behaves. And the more I wrong him the more frightened I think I'm becoming of him because the more reason he has to hate me. So I'll settle the matter by doing something so hideous that he'll *have* to hate me and I'll *have* to be frightened of him. Then I'll see to it that I never see him again.

Of course, every time the woman did see the man she went a little potty. She could see in his eyes the pain she'd caused him and could not accept the responsibility of having caused it. I can imagine Joan Grant saying to her, 'You're guilty as hell. So what? Now pull up your socks.'

Two of the strongest instincts in modern man are the desire for death and the embracement of guilt as if guilt were a loving mother. The alcoholic and the chain-smoker are expressing a desire for as slow and comfortable a death as possible. In some ways, the drug addict is already dead: I have worked, briefly, with a couple of drug addicts and found their auras utterly impenetrable, as if I were trying to influence a photograph of someone who had died in the First World War. There is also a chilliness about the drug addict which reminds one of a corpse. To a lesser extent, guilt-ridden homosexuals give off a chilliness as if, because of idiotic social and moralistic conventions, they longed for death because they could find no proper place in life. The woman whom I have described will remain unreachable by any form of therapy until she exorcizes her own fear of pain. Her lack of self-knowledge leaves her wide open to psychic attack, and in fact she has suffered disturbances on three occasions.

On a recent television talk show, the novelist Edna O'Brien, whom I admire very much, showed up hazily drunk and spoke with low-voiced sexy eloquence about the need to free oneself from restrictions imposed by others. Do this, don't do that; get drunk, don't get drunk; go to church (goddamnit!) but not to

131

this one, to that one; get married and raise seventeen kids. She said that she had come to realize this was all hooey, that one must learn what one truly wants to do and then do it. This is self-exorcism from guilt and it is far more difficult than it sounds because it requires self-knowledge, which is usually painful. Emerson remarked that 'Obey thyself' is the hardest commandment of all.

It is a truism that the exorcist must be a pure and fastidious man. Something or someone told me once in a dream, 'In order to commune with spirits, you must *be* like spirits'. In the Roman Catholic church prayer and confession are recommended before the undertaking of an exorcism. Confession is an excellent idea because the exorcist will then feel that he has been forgiven for his mistakes in the past – or, as I would prefer to put it, that he has forgiven himself.

And yet, in exorcism goodwill towards oneself and the right intentions are the truly essential factors. Strength, presence of mind, willingness to endure pain and the absolute conviction that one will not stop until the operation has been completed are of course *sine quibus non*. But a Roman Catholic priest once told me that Padre Pio, a great modern mystic whom he had met, stank of garlic. I do not doubt, however, that Padre Pio could have performed the rite of exorcism regardless of his state of breath, because he possessed the power that comes of love of the Godhead and acceptance of oneself within it.

Humility and exorcism
The *Shorter Oxford English Dictionary* defines humility as 'the quality of being humble or having a lowly opinion of oneself'. In fact, the opposite is true. Humility and genuine self-respect go hand in hand. A person in need of exorcism or any form of therapy must first have the courage to admit he needs help: this is a gigantic step for most people. One finds oneself coping with a situation in which the mind is intelligent enough to know what it needs, but not brave enough to admit it. Courageous action always indicates that one is willing to stoop; that the all-important 'self' will be sacrificed if necessary. The most courageous man of whom I have ever read ended up stripped, beaten, humiliated and crucified. It is

clear from the gospels that he also had a rather generous measure of self-respect: so much, in fact, that he would not surrender his self for the mere privilege of living among his inferiors. And yet, he gladly washed their feet.

When this humility dawns on a person, he feels a great joy, an expansion of himself which he would not have thought possible. It is as if he could reach out with both hands and touch the antipodes. He is utterly selfless and self-possessed, because he has realized that what he regarded as 'self' is totally illusionary. This false 'self' the exorcist must reject – not without affection, but he must reject it. When 'self' becomes Self recognized as an organism existing within the Godhead, surrounded by It and, if he is an adept, encompassing It as it encompasses him in an act of total and mutual love, then the word 'love' begins to take on true meaning; and no power in creation can threaten it. This is no soppy truism. It is the most difficult task imaginable.

When I was fifteen or so, a student at St Louis University High, I published a poem in the student magazine I had written based largely on my readings of Descartes. *Meditations on First Philosophy* was forbidden, so I was obviously going to hell anyway and didn't see why I shouldn't publish the poem. A gaggle of Jesuit scholastics assembled in a football huddle and emerged with a novena-studded football, consoling telephone calls to my parents and a general reluctance to allow the priests to give me the sacraments. I continued to receive the sacraments, as did Descartes, who after all did dedicate his major work to a bishop. His famous *Cogito ergo sum* was only an echo of St Augustine, so it was difficult, in the long-lost days of youthful clear logic, to see what the fuss was all about. I was pretty stubborn about defending my poem, but was brought down to size, finally. Not by a scholastic: by one of the lay brothers who scrubbed the steps and had read my poem. He had an elfin, secretive quality about him as he tidied up the mess we students made, and it had never occurred to me that he read anything. I was probably pretty condescending until he said something I shall never forget. I thought I had him cornered on the question of perception and the possibility of direct knowledge, when he said: 'It's very

133

simple. All you need is the humility to know.'

If you need help, ask for it. And say thanks.

Two syndromes

Loss of concentration

A common symptom of psychic attack is the inability of the victim to maintain a coherent pattern of thought. Fright begets hysteria, which will not allow the patient to think clearly, because the reality of what is happening to him is too frightening to consider. Guilt, also, plays a part in this. I have frequently thought that a possible factor of failing memory in the aged is connected with guilt: at maturity of insight, one realizes that one has committed various errors. A man may have failed his wife or his children; not achieved his goals; abandoned his ideals; ruined someone's life. These memories are painful, so he rejects them. And because the unconscious is a quick and thorough learner, he begins to reject painless memories as well. A victim of psychic attack may sometimes ramble on aimlessly, like a hit-and-run victim at the tower of Babel; a well-aimed attack plays on both fear and guilt, and both tell the mind to say, 'Forget it. Forget.'

Of course, this syndrome by itself is no criterion for judging whether a person is under psychic attack or not. A bottle of plonk mixed with hard liquor produces the same effect. But forgetfulness, incessant babbling and a glazed expression are frequent results of psychic attack. It is undoubtedly true that many persons now in mental hospitals are not mentally deficient at all, but have either dabbled in the occult with disastrous results to themselves, or become innocent or not-so-innocent victims of psychic attack.

'Funny eyes'

A Muslim whom I met recently is convinced that he is under the influence of the Evil Eye or, as he calls it, the Jealous Eye. All I know of the man is that he has suffered a number of curiously related calamities and is terribly frightened. Unpleasant as it may be, however, the Evil Eye does exist, and it is not impossible that someone has hexed him. (It is even

134

more possible when one considers that he believes in the Jealous Eye. But a hate force can be effective whether the victim believes or not. The question here is whether simple thought is a force and can influence persons or objects for good or ill, even without a person's knowledge. Science tells us it can.)

Trained psychics know immediately when someone is giving them the Evil Eye. An old trick for counteracting it is to concentrate one's gaze not on the attacker's eyes but at a point directly above the bridge of his nose, between the eyes. In effect one is concentrating on the would-be attacker's third eye with all three of one's own: in a psychic punch-up, three is better than two. If you ever have the misfortune to find yourself in the presence of someone whom you feel is truly malevolent and concentrating his hatred on you, leave the room; it is pointless to look for trouble. If, however, such a course of action is awkward or impossible, do the following. Cross your legs, and fold your arms over them or your breast, pretending to relax and rub your shoulders. You may even cross your fingers, if it's not too obvious. This prevents energy from entering or leaving your body. Do *not* let the person fix you in his gaze; this is just what he wants. If you must look at him – he will try to make you do so – concentrate on that spot on his forehead where Indians sometimes paint a dot, which has the effect of jamming the wavelength of the thought he is trying to send out. Continue chattering merrily and if possible say something funny enough to make the whole room of company laugh. The would-be attacker will soon wear himself out. Indeed, he'll wonder what the hell went wrong, unless he knows enough to know what you're doing – then he'll think twice about continuing.

You may try a simple and harmless experiment to prove the efficacy of this technique. If you find yourself on the tube and a rather unsavoury character sitting opposite you is staring at you rather noticeably, concentrate on his third eye. The battle will be won in a matter of seconds.

Willpower in averting psychic attack

In this book I have been discussing some historical facts on the

135

subject of exorcism, spoken with people involved today in the actual practice, cited a few case histories and, hopefully, prepared the reader for what he must do in the unlikely occurrence of genuine psychic attack. All too flippantly, due to lack of space and time, I have discussed some of the basic questions concerning the nature of evil. For practical purposes, I may, for the licensed scholar, have to appear equally puerile on the subject of willpower in dealing with psychic disturbance; but I am concerned here not with academic arguments, merely results.

The meaning of true will, with an emphasis on the true, is not to force yourself to do something that in the end will harm you. The rugby player, or someone who drives a horse almost to its death in the name of courage, does not demonstrate true will. True will is an acceptance of the natural flow of things, a combination of self-knowledge and – hardest of all – obedience to the true self. Now the natural flow of things sometimes seems chaotic, shapeless, frightening. Pascal realized this when he wrote that he was terrified by all these immense silences. The meaning to the psyche of any mythical monster is that one must face the totally unknown, grotesque and unexpected, often when one is least prepared. One must do this, because one exists in a world which one scarcely knows, which is sometimes grotesque, and in which one often finds oneself 'alone and afraid in a world [he] never made'. Every man has his odyssey.

The most difficult thing for a person to accept is his own beauty, his own right to exist. The realization of his own beauty makes him ashamed of the various ways in which he has failed the universe. This results in guilt, repression, often irrational cruelty. In a case of true Redemption, it results in tears. This sense of guilt, resulting, paradoxically, from a sense of one's own beauty, may even make one wish one were dead. The attacker, if he is good at his job, will play on this sense of guilt, an apparent death-wish which is in fact a desire for a more intensified life, as the medieval church writers well knew. They spoke of *suspiria,* 'a deep sigh', 'tears of love', 'these soothing tears', as a realization of one's longing for God. The occultist goes further and says that a longing for God is also a longing for one's true self. Dante spoke truer than he knew when he said, 'In His will is our peace'. Rightly interpreted, this means that we are one and the same as the Godhead, if we but choose to know ourselves and act on the knowledge.

The psychic attacker may be easily foiled by one who truly accepts his own *right to be*. This quality is rarer than may at first appear. It involves a degree of self-knowledge wherein one must weigh one's faults against one's merits, and few indeed are the people prepared to do this in the clear light of reason. Amazingly, many people dwell only on their faults. They cannot see their virtues (*virtutes* in the Latin sense, meaning strengths) and are ripe soil for psychic attack. Anyone who has ever seen or experienced the effects of a domineering mother, a bullying husband or a nagging wife will recognize that the trick of their game is to emphasize the victim's weakness, over and over, night and day if possible, until the poor subject becomes blind to all his good points. This is usually just psychological, but in a case of psychic attack the tactics are often the same.

In dealing with psychic attack, defence is the best offence. The wish to retaliate may be mistaken for 'having a strong will' but it is in fact playing right into the attacker's hands, and anyway not too bright: why play his game according to his rules? Truly willful personalities can absorb and digest a great deal of psychic abuse without raising a finger to protect themselves; they have everything going for them, and they know it.

A Navajo Prayer

Today I will walk out
in the air, my element,
as fishes walk out
in the water.

Today I will breathe deeply
in my element.
Today
all evil will flee
at the sight of my body.

Today I will be
as I always have been.
A blue light
will be in my body.

I will have a light body.

Today I will be happy
forever.
Nothing can stop it.

I walk with beauty
                    before me
I walk with beauty
                    behind me
I walk with beauty
                    below me
I walk with beauty
                    above me
I walk with beauty
                    all around me.

My words
will be beautiful.

In beauty
it is finished.

138

A word to the future

What is needed, obviously, urgently, is one trained exorcist in every Christian diocese, every Witch coven and every religious organization, working in close connection with a physician and a qualified psychiatrist. At the moment, hot as the subject is, this prospect seems depressingly remote. Exorcism is neither a myth nor the romanticized adventure story described in *The Exorcist* but a very real experience, as anyone who has been exorcised will tell you. It is no joke. Until the above conditions exist, books like this one will have to be written.

Appendix: Dissociation and hallucination

When I had finished this book I was invited to do various interviews with the media. It occurred to me then that I had taken a rather staunch position, however unwittingly, in which I was assuming that my readers would not only know what I was writing about but admit, if only for the sake of argument, that exorcism was an acceptable form of therapy. The interviews convinced me that, in offering the reader my own evidence and supporting it with that of others who had had extensive experience with exorcisms, I was doing him some disservice. I believe that psychic attack and possession are not only possible but occur in an alarming number of cases. So do a substantial number of GPs and psychiatrists. This is a difficult pill for many to swallow; if it is true it is frightening and distressing because it upsets the 'scientific' convictions of a goodly number of dedicated lifetimes. I thought it might be illuminating to play my own Devil's Advocate and state the case against possession – at least, the one I find most convincing.

Quite by chance, as *Exorcism* was almost finished, I came across a fascinating book by Dr M. J. Field,* whose main contention was that Biblical 'angels' were not spirits at all but a sect of monks who practised good works, asceticism and what occultists call Hermeticism, or the practice of mental discipline, spiritual development and bodily control to produce 'magical' results. Dr Field amassed nearly forty years' experience in West Africa observing instances of spirit possession among the tribes of Ghana. He cited, very convincingly, two explanations which psychology has offered for this phenomenon.

* *Angels and Ministers of Grace*, Longman, 1971.

140

'Spirit possession' is a perfectly natural phenomenon depending on the mental mechanism known to psychology as *dissociation* (p.65).

Dr Field regards dissociation as a split which occurs not in the personality, but in the 'possessed' individual's consciousness.

> In the dissociated state the everyday 'stream of consciousness' is split into parallel streams, one of which possesses the entire field of awareness, the rest being temporarily obliterated ... Anyone who drives a car knows that one part of his mind looks after the driving 'automatically' while the rest ranges freely. But in this everyday experience the separated streams can be brought instantly back into one at the demand of the moment. In the dissociated state of mind the familiar stream of awareness goes into abeyance – into sleep, if you will – and a split-off stream takes control (pp.66–7).

This is Dr Field's explanation of the phenomenon of possession. According to him there is no invading entity to trouble the patient, only a temporary loss of one part of his consciousness. So far from being 'possessed', he has been *dis*possessed of part of his waking faculty.

> When the person comes out of this dissociated state he does not remember what the split-off part of his mind did, or made him do, under the eyes of his neighbours, during the episode (p.67).

Dr Field would have been the first to admit that the mind unleashed has strange powers over the physical body; and he argued that such feats as walking barefoot over hot coals, showing the strength of seven normal men and so on, are due entirely to the occurrence of dissociation. He makes a distinction between hallucination, which is usually associated with hysteria, and feels that dissociation is not 'any more pathological than sleep'. But hallucination, too, is a valid explanation for 'possession'.

141

Of all the non-occult explanations for the occurrence of possession this seems to me the most interesting. It does not attempt to deny the phenomenon itself, which many persons have attempted to do. And it is simple, as feasible scientific explanations are. Yet it seems to me to beg the question. Dr Field's experience of possession is limited to observations he has made of African tribesmen, and he makes no mention of occurrences in Europe. Also, it is difficult for me to agree that the case of John Taylor, or the murders committed under the influence of Charles Manson, are syndromes no 'more pathological than sleep'. Any form of therapy that has proved itself helpful in limiting the frequency of such occurrences is deserving of more than a shrug, a condescending smile and a nod of dismissal.

Select bibliography

All of these works have proved quite useful to me, but a comprehensive list of works on exorcism would be the length of this book by itself, so I make no pretence of having covered the field here. Many of these books are interesting for their treatment of subjects other than exorcism.

BARDON, FRANZ. *Initiation into Hermetics*. Dieter Rüggeberg, Wuppertal, West Germany, 1971.

CAVENDISH, RICHARD. *The Black Arts*. Routledge & Kegan Paul, London, 1967.

CONWAY DAVID. *Magic: An Occult Primer*. Johnathan Cape, London, 1972.

CROWLEY, ALEISTER. *Magick in Theory And Practice*. Castle Books, New York, originally published 1929.

FORTUNE, DION. *Through the Gates of Death*. Aquarian Press, London, 1968.

– *Psychic Self-Defence*. Aquarian Press, Northamptonshire, 1974.

GARDNER, GERALD. *The Meaning of Witchcraft*. Aquarian Press, London, 1971.

GARDNER, RICHARD. *The Tarot Speaks*. Tandem, London, 1971.

GRANT, JOAN. *Winged Pharaoh*. Methuen, London, 1937.

– *Many Lifetimes*. Doubleday, New York, 1967.

HUGHES, PENNETHORPE. *Witchcraft*. Penguin, Harmondsworth, 1971.

HUSON, PAUL. *Mastering Witchcraft*. Corgi, London, 1972.

– *The Devil's Picture Book*. Sphere Books, London, 1972.

JUNG, CARL. *The Archetype and the Collective Unconscious.* Routledge & Kegan Paul, London, 1971.

KERR, JOHN STEVENS. *The Mystery and Magic of the Occult.* SCM Press, 1971.

KOCH, KURT. *Demonology Past And Present.* Kregel Publications, Michigan, 1973.

LAVEY, ANTON SZANDOR. *The Satanic Bible.* Avon Books, New York, 1969.

LEVI, ELIPHAS. *The Key of the Mysteries.* Rider, London, 1969.

LOYOLA, IGNATIUS (ST). *Spiritual Exercises.* Trans. Thomas Corbishley, S. J. Anthony Clarke, Hertfordshire, 1973.

MOREL, R., and WALTER, S. *Conjurations et Sortiléges.* Bibliothéque Marabout, Paris, 1964.

NEIL-SMITH, CHRISTOPHER. *The Exorcist and the Possessed.* James Pike Ltd, Cornwall, 1974.

PARACELSUS. *The Archidoxes of Magic.* Askin Publishers, London, 1975.

PETITPIERRE, DOM ROBERT (ed.). *Exorcism.* SPCK, London, 1975.

RHODES, N.T.F. *The Satanic Mass.* Arrow Books, London, 1973.

SHAH, IDRIES. *The Secret Lore of Magic.* Abacus, London, 1972.

STRACHAN, FRANÇOISE. *Casting Out the Devils.* Aquarian Press, London, 1972.

RAVENSDALE, TOM, and MORGAN, JAMES. *The Psychology of Witchcraft.* John Bartholomew & Son Ltd, Edinburgh, 1974.